Originally published in 1867
First published 2014

Amberley Publishing
The Hill, Stroud
Gloucestershire, GL5 4EP

www.amberley-books.com

Copyright © Amberley Publishing, 2014

The right of Amberley Publishing to be identified as the Author
of this work has been asserted in accordance with the
Copyrights, Designs and Patents Act 1988.

British Library Cataloguing in Publication Data.
A catalogue record for this book is available from the British Library.

ISBN 978 1 4456 4339 7 (print)
ISBN 978 1 4456 4347 2 (ebook)

Typeset in 10pt on 12pt Sabon.
Typesetting and Origination by Amberley Publishing.
Printed in the UK.

Contents

Introduction by the Editor

Welsh cooking traditions go back centuries. Beef and dairy cattle are raised widely. Sheep farming is extensive in the country and lamb is the meat traditionally associated with Welsh cooking, particularly in dishes such as roast lamb with fresh mint sauce. The leek, as something of the nation's 'national' vegetable, also features prominently. Welsh cooking often includes seafood, especially close to the coast, where fishing culture is strong and fisheries are common.

In this, the quintessential Welsh cook book, the Right Honorable Lady Llanover, following a meeting with 'the Welsh hermit of the Cell of St Gover', explores traditional Welsh cuisine from the turn of the century, with an excellent range of homemade recipes such as South Wales Salmon, Welsh Mutton Chops, Welsh Leek Broth and Welsh Cakes. Also included are a number of domestic or household tips and tricks, recorded in the 'Traveller's Notebook' at the end of the book.

Introduction to the Original Edition

GENTLE READER,

As the present work is intended for the especial benefit of those of *gentle* birth who may not have any very extensive knowledge of economy in domestic practice, and as the Hero of the accompanying annals belonged to the last century, the commencement of this Introductory Epistle is not misplaced; and the Author has adopted the present form, including dialogue remarks, annotations, and explanations, from experience of facts, which tend to prove that the multiplication of Cookery Books on the common plan has very little increased the amount of knowledge of the fundamental principles of the real art of Cookery and Domestic Economy. Whether the Master of the Cell of Gover will be more successful than his predecessors in awakening the minds of the present generation to the necessity of understanding themselves what ought to be done, and what avoided, to ensure a well-cooked dish, time alone will show !——but if *the Hermit* only convinces a few persons, who desire to benefit their fellow-creatures, that those who want food might be benefited to an enormous extent, were it not for the ignorance of the majority of those who have enough, in matters of practical utility, the knowledge of which would prevent the destruction of millions of tons of the best food, this little book will not have been written in vain.

The Author has received, for the last few years, numerous inquiries and applications, from friends, for information about certain simple dishes, which they had, in the course of their travels, tasted at the board of her friend the Hermit of Gover's Cell, and these applications have now increased to such an extent, that, finding it impossible to reply to them satisfactorily, a promise was given of "*a Book*," the appearance of which has been hastened by recent urgent demands for a receipt, *How to make a Cook?*

The Author does not profess to write a Tale. The present little volume is for the avowed purpose of instruction in Cookery, Domestic Economy, and other matters involving home comfort, for which the narrative is merely a vehicle. Where quantities are mentioned, they have been generally extracted and translated from a day-book, kept in Welsh by the Hermit's first hand (Gwenllian, the senior widow), which day-book was made from original Welsh memoranda in white chalk, on the door of the Larder, made by Marged, the Hermit's second hand, as the materials were weighed, and their proceeds afterwards measured.

The Author feels that no apology is necessary for making public practical instructions which are the result of many years' individual experience, in matters *universally admitted* to require an *entire reform*, which are very little understood by the poor, and *still less* comprehended by the rich. It is, however, fair to the

Author, that the " *Gentle Readers* " should be informed (whether male or female), that, had time and circumstances permitted, this book would have been more complete, but, under the impression that *facts* will constitute its chief value, the Author decided on publishing one volume as quickly as possible, without waiting to rearrange the subjects or to improve the composition, being very certain that, *if* there is *any value* to be found in its pages, other persons will be awakened to their own practical responsibilities and to the knowledge of practical possibilities by what the Welsh Hermit has begun.

AUG^A LLANOVER.

Recipes

BOILED FOWL.

WEIGHT of fowl, three and a half lbs. ; a quarter of a pint of cold water to each pound. Fill the outer vessel with water, and let it simmer very slowly for two hours and a quarter, unless the meat of the fowl is tender and fit for eating sooner, which can be proved by trying it with a fork. Pour off the broth, which ought to be about a pint of strong chicken broth, and when cold will be a jelly. The bones of the chicken, after the meat is eaten (or all taken off), are to be broken up, and stewed in a digester for two or three hours, with a pint of water to every pound of bones; then pour the liquor off, which ought to produce about half a pint of jelly, and the bones are to be re-broken, and put into the digester again, with a pint of water to every pound of bones, which will, of course, weigh *less* than before the first stewing. They are to remain between one and two hours stew-ing, then pour off the liquor, which ought to produce more than a quarter of a pint of jelly. The bones to be broken the third time, and subjected to the same process, with a pint of water to the pound, their weight being again diminished: the liquor ought to produce a quarter of a pint of jelly. Thus, a fowl or three pounds and a half weight will, under proper management, on an average, produce, *besides the meat*, more than a quart of jelly stock, first and last, including the pint produced by the first boiling.

N.B.—It must be remembered that slight differences as to produce will be found, according to the sort, the quality, or condition of poultry, as well as butcher's meat: but the receipts given in this work have been written down from actual practical experiments, often repeated, and the variations in the produce are, on an average, trifling, excepting where the meat has been *very fat*, and when that is the case in butcher's meat, the same quantity of jelly stock must *never* be expected as when the meat is lean, inasmuch as the fat will *not* produce gravy; consequently, when there is a great overplus of fat, less water should be allowed to the weight of meat.

In the proceeds from the Hermit's fowl, the oil on the top of the jelly from the first boiling measured a quarter of a pint, and the fat collected from the surface of all the jellies amounted to a quarter of a pint.

Total produce of Hermit's fowl (*besides the meat*) :—

> Jelly stock, 1 quart.
> Oil ,, $\frac{1}{4}$ of a pint.
> Fat ,, $\frac{1}{4}$ of a pint.

— · ———

PARSLEY SAUCE FOR BOILED FOWL.

Two ounces of fresh butter, cut in little bits, put into a double saucepan, with as much flour as will make it into a stiff paste ; then add two tablespoonfuls of milk ; stir well, add six tablespoonfuls of water, continue to stir till it is quite hot and the thickness of good cream. The above is *now* plain melted butter, and ready for parsley sauce, which must be made by previously having had the parsley washed very clean, and picking every leaf off the stems ; put a small teaspoonful of salt into half a pint of boiling water, boil the parsley in this for ten minutes, drain it on a sieve, mince it fine, or bruise it to a pulp, and stir it into the melted butter prepared as above described.

FRICASEED COLD CHICKEN.—(Page 33.)

Chop very fine leek-roots, celery, a small quantity of turnip, and some persons like a *little* carrot. Put the whole into a saucepan with sufficient top fat (if from chicken stock *all the better*) to form a thick pulp when thoroughly incorporated with the chopped vegetables (the whole of the vegetables together being about two ounces), stir briskly over the fire for ten minutes; then shake in as much flour as will make it a stiff paste, stirring well for five minutes longer, then put the whole into a double saucepan in which is three-quarters of a pint of chicken stock, which has been previously warmed, and after well stirring, again leave it to stew slowly for three-quarters of an hour, then pass the whole through a wire sieve into a basin, and pour what is strained back into the double, adding two tablespoonfuls of cream, after which the flavour must be improved as required, by stirring round a sprig of orange thyme, or any other herb wanted, and, if the flavour of celery and onions is not sufficient, it is now to be increased by stirring round pieces of either of those vegetables, and taking them out as soon as sufficient taste is obtained. The meat of the cold chicken is to be cut or pulled into long pointed pieces, and put into the sauce, where, being well stirred, it is to remain until thoroughly warmed through, and the chicken flavour imparted to the sauce. This will take a few minutes more or less according to the heat to which the hot water on the outside is exposed,—the slower the better, as, if the water is kept fiercely* boiling instead of barely simmering, the chicken will be beat to pieces; whereas having already been once dressed, it ought only to be done the second time sufficiently to have the chicken flavour imparted to the sauce, and the flavour of the sauce absorbed by the chicken.

In the Hermit's mode of cookery in separate double vessels, any dishes can be kept warm without injury for a long while, should the dinner by any accident be retarded.*

---

* The reader of this recipe, who may possibly be acquainted with the copper tray called a Bain-Marie, to hold hot water, which is used by professed cooks to keep their sauces from burning, and may probably suppose that that contrivance was *unknown* to the Hermit, and that *his* system of double vessels for cookery was only a clumsy substitution for a scientific invention, beyond his knowledge or his reach ; it is, therefore, necessary to add, that it was in consequence of the *total inefficiency* of the copper tray, called a Bain-Marie, to effect the objects which it was the ambition of the Hermit to attain, that he discarded the Bain-Marie altogether, as an expensive and cumbersome addition to his kitchen, which took up a great deal of room, and did very little work. and was totally inadmissible where there was not a very large stove.

No. II.

ROAST LEG OF MUTTON.

Leg of mutton weighing five lbs.; put on the hook attached to the yarn, which hangs from a crank (see page 40), 24 inches from the fire, basted with clarified dripping, or suet. Keep an earthen pan on the bottom of the screen next the dripping-pan; after basting, ladle all the gravy, or liquid fat, out of the dripping-pan into the earthen pan, from which it can be taken as often as needed to baste, and again returned. A leg of mutton of this size will take about three hours; half an hour before it is finished, put it four inches nearer the fire; put half a pint of boiling water in a watering-pot with the rose on, salt to taste, and pour over the joint slowly, which will produce a great increase of gravy, and when browned again after the watering, and well basted, sprinkle flour all over it with a flour dredger, and again baste to froth it. The gravy to be served with the meat should, if possible, have been saved from a previous joint, and warmed in a double saucepan; but, if not practicable, the gravy should be taken out of the dripping-pan after the watering, and placed in a basin or dish to cool, and when the fat is sufficiently congealed to be removed, the clear gravy can be rewarmed in a double saucepan, and would be ready to be served with the meat by the time it is frothed and dished.

JELLY FROM THE BONES OF ROAST LEGS OF WELSH MUTTON.

The bones of roast Welsh legs of mutton, broken small, and put in a digester with three pints of water, produced a pint and a half of jelly after stewing slowly for three hours; the bones being re-broken and put down again with a pint and a half of water, after stewing for two hours produced three-quarters of a pint more jelly. The bones being broken the third time, and put down with one pint of water, produced one-quarter pint more jelly. Total quantity of jelly from a pound and a half of leg of mutton bones, two pints and a half.

No. III.

STEWED BEEF.

Trimmings of half-rounds of beef cut in pieces for pies, 6 lbs.

Brisket, stewed same time, 15 lbs.

Beef altogether, 21 lbs.

Onions, celery, leeks, turnips, and carrots about four soup-plates full, a soup-plate holding about 1 lb. of chopped vegetables.   Suet, or top fat, 1 lb.

N.B.—The suet or top fat which is added to stewed beef to make it more mellow, should always be added the last thing over the vegetables, because otherwise it would prevent the juice and flavour of the vegetables from penetrating into the meat.

Water two quarts and one pint, being a quarter of a pint of water to every pound of beef.   Stewed in double vessel for twelve hours, produced six quarts of stock, which when cold was a strong jelly; and the fat when cold taken off the top weighed two pounds and a half.

It must always be remembered that the fatter the meat the less stock will be produced; nothing is so wasteful or unwholesome for household purposes as over-fat meat, or fat produced by oil-cake and forcing feeding, and such animals are, moreover, scarcely ever free from disease.

The sauce for this stewed beef (if eaten hot) is prepared from its own jelly stock in the same manner as hashed mutton, with addition of turnip and carrot balls (or shreds) stewed till tender in broth.   (See page 64.)

No. IV.

HASHED MUTTON.

Cut as much mutton as is required from the remainder of a roast leg in pointed pieces.* Fry one ounce and a half of onion, and the same of celery chopped fine, and one ounce of turnip, with a sufficient quantity of fresh top fat, cut in small pieces, from soup or broth, stirred round and round over a stove or fire in a clean tin saucepan for ten minutes; then add as much flour as will stiffen it into a paste of the consistency of wet mortar, and stir round and round over the stove for five minutes more; then add a sufficient quantity of the jelly from the bone of the leg of roast mutton, to be of the consistence of thick pea-soup; then pour the whole into a double saucepan, in the outside of which there must be a sufficient quantity of boiling water to fill within an inch of the top of the inner saucepan. Let the whole simmer gently for a quarter of an hour or twenty minutes; then pour through a wire sieve and return into a clean double saucepan, which replace on the stove; taste, and if it requires any further flavouring of herbs or vegetables, add them; then put in the prepared pieces of meat, stir well, and let it remain in a very slow heat for half an hour, when it will be ready for the table.

———— ·· ——— ————

No. V.

SIMPLE WHITE SOUP.

One pint of veal stock and one pint of brown stock in a large basin; place the basin over a saucepan of boiling water on a stove or fire, add an onion cut in half, three or four pieces of celery slit in variousplaces to let out the juice, a sprig or two of basil and marjory (if in winter these herbs may be used in powder, having been bottled * in the summer); place a plate over the top of the basin, and the lid of the saucepan on the plate to keep in the heat; let all simmer together, the water in the saucepan being kept boiling under the basin for forty minutes; then add four tablespoonfuls of cream and macaroni cut small, after having been previously stewed till tender in mutton broth or veal stock.

————————

THE WHITE SOUP OF GOVER.

Put one quart of veal stock in a double saucepan to warm, then chop fine six ounces of onion, six of celery, four of leeks, six of pumpkin, four of carrots; stir the whole in a single saucepan over the stove for ten minutes, with as much top fat as will make them into a pulp, without burning or being oily; then shake in with the dredger as much flour as will form the whole into a pulpy *paste*, stirring briskly for five minutes more; then add the whole mass to the hot veal stock in the double saucepan, and let all stew slowly together surrounded with boiling water for an hour and a half, frequently stirring; then pass through a wire sieve, return into a clean double saucepan, add whatever flavouring is deficient, either in salt or herbs, with six spoonfuls of cream; let the whole be well stirred and thoroughly hot, and it is ready for the table.

N.B.—More or less cream can be added according to taste, and it is better flavoured if the cream is added before it is put through the wire sieve, to which some persons may object for reasons given by the Hermit; * but whether before or after, an additional

flavour of herbs is generally required, and sometimes
more onion after the cream, which can be done by
adding pieces of vegetables or sprigs of herbs until
the additional flavour has been obtained, when th:y
can be taken out before it is served.

N.B.—The stocks used for the above soups are
the jelly produced by boiling or stewing in a double
vessel either veal or beef, till in perfection for eating (as described by the Hermit), in the proportions
of a quarter pint of water to one lb. of meat (bone
and flesh together); if very fat, less stock will be
produced.—*Nothing is worse economy than overplus of
fat.* When *broth* only is wanted *half* a pint of water
to the pound may be used.

THE HERMIT'S GRAVY SOUP.*

Five pounds of lean beef cut in small pieces,
(trimmed from the inside of two half-rounds before
they were salted,) fifteen pounds of brisket of beef,
four pounds of onions, leeks, turnips, and carrots, all
finely chopped, in the proportions of one pound of
onions, one pound of celery, half a pound of leeks,
quarter of a pound of turnips, quarter of a pound of

carrots. Suet one pound, water two quarts and one pint, being a quarter of a pint to every pound of meat, stewed in double twelve hours, by which time the meat was not overdone, but very tender and juicy. The produce was five quarts and a pint and a half of stock, which when cold was a clear jelly; fat taken off the jelly when cold weighed two pounds and a half.

N.B.—Had the meat been fatter the produce of soup would have been much less, and there would have been waste in eating the meat from disproportion of fat to the lean. The arrangement of the meat, &c. in the inside vessel, was as follows:— First, brisket; then the trimmings on the top of the brisket; second, vegetables; third, a sprinkling of salt on the vegetables; fourth, suet also on the vegetables. By attention to this order of things, the juices of the vegetables drawn out by slightly salting are distilled through the meat, while the suet is also slowly melted, and enriches the meat as it passes through; the superabundance, after the meat is saturated, is all again collected from the top of the jelly stock when cold. By this process of slow cooking in a double vessel two very important objects are gained; the first being the *impossibility* of *burning* or *entirely spoiling* the meat *or the soup;* the second, that more soup is obtained than the quantity of water which is put to the meat; whereas upon the old system *much less* soup is produced than the quantity of water put in, because the liquor is *boiled away* and *wasted*. The trimmings thus cooked make the best beef family pies, the bottom part of the jelly stock being used for the gravy, which not being so transparent as the upper part is not so well adapted in appearance for gravy soup, but is especially savoury and well-flavoured. The brisket itself is ready to be served next day, with the sauce recommended by the Hermit.* *No skimming* while hot is *ever* required for *any of the recipes in this book.*

The gravy soup, as well as other soups, will generally require some extra flavouring of herbs and vegetables when warmed for the table, which warming must always be in a double saucepan, or a basin over a saucepan of boiling water: the *latter* is the most delicate.

--- --- ---

No. VI.

HASHED MUTTON (SIMPLE).

Prepare the cold mutton as directed in No. 4; salt it slightly, flour it lightly, turning it well over with two forks; put it into a double saucepan, with a sufficient quantity of jelly from the bones of mutton previously flavoured with onion and herbs; let the meat remain in this sauce in a gentle heat, frequently stirred for three quarters of an hour before it is served. If there is no jelly from mutton bones, clear gravy from roast mutton, similarly flavoured, would be very good.

No. VII.

MUTTON PIE.

Neck or loin of mutton, five pounds, cut in chops, put in a double saucepan with *half a quarter* of a pint of water to the pound; add one pound of vegetables chopped fine (onions and celery equal quantities, turnips and carrots half the quantity); a sprinkling of salt. Stew for two hours; when the meat is sufficiently tender, take it off, pour the liquor into a basin to cool, and cut the meat off the bones, removing also the superfluous fat. When the liquor is cold take the solid fat off the top, and the stock will then be in a jelly; add this jelly to the meat which has been cut off the bones, and place the whole in a thick crockery basin over a saucepan of boiling water until the jelly has melted amongst the meat, and the whole is warmed through; then remove till the next day, when the meat will be imbedded in the jelly which will have cooled round it, and of which it will have absorbed a great deal. The meat and jelly can then be placed in layers in the pie-dish, and there ought to be (if done properly) considerably more jelly than is required for gravy for the pie, which overplus is to be kept back; a little fresh parsley chopped small is to be sprinkled between the meat.

The paste for the pie is to be made with six ounces of flour, three ounces of the top fat, taken off the mutton jelly, and put on the fire in a saucepan with a quarter of a pint of water; when the water boils make a hole in the middle of the flour and pour in the boiling water and mutton fat by degrees, mixing the fat in with a spoon; when well mixed, knead it till of the proper stiffness, and dredge the board with flour to make it smooth; cover your pie, make a hole in the top, and form a little ornament with a small stem to fit into it. Fill your baking tin with water under the pie-dish to prevent too great a heat to the bottom: when the paste is baked the pie is done. Screw out the top ornament and pour in as much liquid mutton jelly as the pie can receive, which must be previously warmed in a double saucepan; replace the ornament, and serve the pie.

N.B.—A pie after baking will always take a good deal of extra gravy, but it will not take nearly all that the meat has produced when properly done, and of which there ought to be more to spare, which can be used for soups or sauces, or added to mutton broth.

No. VIII.
PEA-SOUP (WINTER).

One pint of peas soaked in the well for twenty-four hours; stew three hours in a double saucepan with one pint of bone stock, and a quarter of a pound of finely-chopped onions, and a quarter of a pound of celery; rub through a wire sieve, put back again into the double, add one pint and a half of good broth or stock, and stew one hour more, with one onion split in half, and three pieces of split celery, and a little fresh or powdered basil; add salt and powdered or fresh mint, with marjory, and orange thyme to taste. The above soup may be varied by adding a quarter of a pint of cream before the last onion and herbs are put in; and the Hermit occasionally had rice stewed in new milk in a double saucepan, and added instead of the cream, on which occasion fried bread was not served, which was done when the pea-soup was made without rice.

No. IX.

GREEN PEA-SOUP (SUMMER).

Chop all together *very* small, three lettuces, two cucumbers, half a pound of spinach, half a pound of onions, half a pound of leeks. Let them be stirred in a single saucepan for ten minutes with a quarter of a pound of fresh top fat from beef stock until in a pulp; meantime, have prepared in another double a pint and a half of veal or beef jelly stock from stewed beef or boiled veal, also one pint of old green peas, which have also been stewed and pulped through a wire sieve; add to the stock the pulp of the peas and other vegetables; flavour according to taste, by stirring round at last pieces of split celery, a little basil and mint to taste, and serve, having a quarter of a pint of young and tender peas ready boiled to throw in before it is served up. The Hermit sometimes added pieces of cucumber about an inch long, which had been previously stewed in beef or veal jelly stock.

N.B.—Two pounds of green pea-shells chopped or pounded, will produce excellent pea-soup, treated in the same manner as the old green peas in the above recipe, and will be found very convenient when peas are scarce.

***

No. X.

BEEF-STEAK. ·

Place beef-steaks in a large single saucepan, or stew-pan, over the stove ; turn them about until browned on both sides *without being burnt*, with an ounce of top fat from beef stock ; take about two dozen of button onions, and boil till tender, in as much water as will cover them, in a double saucepan; then take the beef-steaks, (about five pounds,) and, when browned, put them with the gravy that has been extracted, into a double, and add to them the water which has boiled the button onions, two ounces of celery chopped small, one ounce of carrots ditto, two ounces of onions ditto ; let the steaks stew with the above from one to two hours, or till tender, then put into a basin, pour all their gravy over them, straining the vegetables out, and leave them till the next day, when the fat, which will have congealed on the top, is to be removed, and the basin with the steaks and gravy placed on a saucepan of boiling water to warm, and if the button onions are liked, they can be added ; also a quarter of a pound of potatoes, cut in little balls or dice, are to be fried in a quarter of a pound of top fat, of a golden yellow, a quarter of an hour before they are wanted. They are to be put on a doubled clean cloth upon a flat dish, and placed in the screen before the kitchen fire, being turned to remove all superfluous fat, and being perfectly hot and dry, are to be put into the gravy with the steaks when served.

No. XI.

TO PRESERVE GAME OR POULTRY, OR ANY SORT OF MEAT, WHEN REQUIRED TO BE KEPT LONG BEFORE IT IS EATEN.

Roast the poultry or game exactly the same as if it was to be eaten immediately ; by the time it is ready have a sufficient quantity of fresh suet (beef is preferred) melted in a double saucepan, put the game or poultry into a pan or vessel sufficiently deep, and pour in *hot suet* till over the top ; keep in a cold place, and when wanted, cut it out of the suet, which will easily be broken off the game, and place the birds in a basin with a very *little* pure broth under them, put the basin over a saucepan of boiling water, cover with a plate, and as soon as the birds have slowly been warmed through, during which process they must be turned, they are ready for the table, with the addition of some pure gravy from something similar, or else from roast mutton. The suet which has melted into the broth will congeal on the top when cold, and can be taken off.

N.B.—It is seldom remembered that dressing meat, *after* it is tainted, will not remove the taint, though it may render it less offensive and unwholesome; consequently, those who wish to preserve meat, game, or poultry in hot weather, must dress it *before* it is tainted.

No. XII.

BAKED FILLET OF VEAL.

Stuff the fillet with stuffing made of finely chopped suet, lemon-peel, and bread crumbs, leek root finely chopped, a little orange thyme, nutmeg, pepper, and salt, pounded with one egg; after it is filleted and stuffed, put two ounces suet or fresh top fat from stock of soups (veal the best) on the top of the fillet after placing it in the iron (outer) part of Ffwrn fach without the inner tin. Place over it (if to be had) a piece of the rind from cold boiled pork, with about a quarter of an inch of the fat adhering to it; add one quart of water, put in an oven of steady heat, not sharp, and *take out* all the fire from under the oven as soon as it is in. A fillet of veal of seven pounds will take about three hours. When done, the gravy must be poured off, and when cold will be in a firm jelly.

N.B.—If the veal was baked in the tin double of the Ffwrn fach, in addition to the outer vessel itself, it would produce more *gravy*, but the objection to this mode of cooking is that the veal will not then *brown outside*; but if the fillet is only wanted for eating cold, for mince veal, &c., or making the Hermit's pies, it had better be done in a double vessel to produce more gravy, and the meat will taste equally good or better. If required to be eaten hot, it can be served next day warmed in a double, with some of its own gravy.

No. XIII.

TONGUE BOILED.

One of the Hermit's salt* tongues, which weighed two pounds, stewed six hours in a double saucepan, with one quart and one pint of spring water, and six ounces of fresh suet. When done the tongue was tender but firm, and the water in which it was boiled being kept till cold, all the suet that had not been absorbed by the tongue was taken off from the surface when solid.

TONGUE ROASTED.

A favourite Welsh dish, and a very excellent one. Wash a fresh tongue well, and when quite clean cut off no more of the roots than will make it stand well on the dish; chop fine equal parts of onions and celery, and half as much of carrots and turnips, and pile them all along the tongue; sprinkle freely with salt, and add half a pound of fresh top fat from soups, or (if not to be had) use chopped suet, but the former is best; then bind up the tongue, with the vegetables and the fat upon it, in two or three folds of thin *" whity brown "* paper, which must be tied on. The tongue is then ready for roasting, and must be well basted, the paper being previously thoroughly greased. A short time before it is done, cut the string, take off the paper, and brown it before it is taken down. The best gravy is that from roast beef, but roast mutton is also suitable. It is customary to stick in a few cloves round the top before it is sent to table, but this is more ornamental than useful.

No. XIV.

HERMIT'S RABBIT FRICASEE.

Two rabbits cut up, weighing four pounds and a half; one pint and half a quarter pint of water, stewed for three hours, produced a pint and a half of jelly. Put away for the next day, then take the pint and a half of rabbit jelly and put on in a double, with two ounces of onions and the same of celery, chopped *very fine*, and a pint and a half of milk; let it stew altogether for half an hour; then put in the rabbit, which has been previously cut in moderate sized pieces, and floured, and let all stew together in the double, frequently stirring, for an hour, slow heat.

If a richer and more delicate dish is required, the vegetables should be stirred over a stove, in a single saucepan, for ten minutes, and then made into a paste with flour, and stirred for five minutes more, and the whole put into a "double" with the rabbit jelly and a little new milk or cream, and after being stirred half an hour put through a wire sieve, returned to the double, then put in the pieces of rabbit for half an hour before serving, which in this case should not be floured.

No. XV.

HERMIT'S BOILED SHOULDER OF MUTTON.

Weighed three pounds; onions, half a pound; celery, half a pound, chopped fine; marjory and a small sprig of orange thyme.

Put in a double with one pint and a half of water, and water boiling round for two hours and a half. Produced one quart of good broth, the meat being tender and juicy.

———

ONION SAUCE FOR BOILED SHOULDER OF MUTTON.

Cut up four onions and stew in a double with a little water till tender; then pour off the water and mix half an ounce of flour with it; then add half a pint of milk, and stir well till of a proper consistency, then pass through the wire sieve and return into the double saucepan; stir well, and when quite hot it is ready to pour over the boiled shoulder of mutton or over boiled rabbits.

No. XVI.

HERMIT'S SAUSAGES.

Quarter of a pound of roast or baked pork, quarter of a pound of baked veal, two ounces of cold boiled tongue, an ounce and a half of onions chopped very fine, an ounce and a quarter of sage, flour well, add pepper and salt to taste; pound well in a mortar, and make into very thin, short, round sausages; beat up one egg well, and glaze the sausages with it, then roll them in two ounces of fine bread crumbs, and fry in boiling-hot top fat (from soup stock) until the sausages are a fine golden brown: if they are at all greasy, put them on a soft hot cloth on a flat dish in a screen before the fire, and turn them on the cloth till they are perfectly dry, before serving.

N.B.—Where pork is used it can be baked in the same manner as directed for the fillet of veal; but if no more is wanting than the quantity to make sausages, it is better to cut up a quarter of a pound of raw pork and a quarter of a pound of raw veal, and half a quarter of a pint of water and a little salt, which can be baked slowly in a double Ffwrn fach, or it can be stewed in a double saucepan till the meat is fit for eating. When it is not convenient to provide pork or veal, cold stewed beef, or indeed any cold meat, will make very good sausages, if pounded, with the addition of a little finely-chopped suet, and well flavoured with sage.

No. XVII.

THE HERMIT'S COLD VEAL PIE.

Bake (or stew in a double) a pound and a half of veal, with not quite a pint of water, and a little orange thyme, some small bits of fresh lemon-peel, and a very small bit of mace. Bake or stew till the veal is in good eating order; it will take more or less time, according to the tenderness of the meat, but, whether baked or stewed, it must be done *very slowly*. When done pour off the gravy, which will become a jelly, and put the meat away till the next day; then pound the veal very fine in a mortar, with a sufficient quantity of boiled salt tongue to give it sufficient saltness and flavour; moisten while pounding with as much of the jelly stock from the veal as will make it into a stiff paste, the consistency of mortar; rub the inside of the dish well with olive oil or top fat; then stick small pieces of dry vermicelli all over the bottom of the dish; line the dish (over the vermicelli) with paste—(the same paste as that in the recipe given for mutton pie)—then put in the pounded meat, press down close and *flat* to the top of the dish, and cover over with the same paste. Bake for an hour in a slow oven with water in the baking-tin under the dish, and when cold it will turn out of the dish *topsy-turvy*, the vermicelli adhering to the paste: when eaten the end should be cut off straight, and slices taken off from one end to the other. The above pie is also excellent for sandwiches.

No. XVIII.

SALT DUCK.

For a common-sized duck, a quarter of a pound of salt, to be well rubbed in and re-rubbed, and turned on a dish every day for three days; then wash all the salt off clean, put it into· a double with half a pint of water to the pound, and let it simmer steadily for two hours. Salt boiled duck, with white onion sauce, is much better than roast duck.

No. XIX.

GREEN PEA-SOUP.
See Appendix No. IX.

No. XX.

ROOT OF TONGUE SOUP.

Cut off the roots of a fresh tongue, wash well in separate waters, and then leave them to soak in a pan sunk in a stone trough or well over which fresh water is constantly running, for half an hour, then take them out and place them in the inner tin of a Ffwrn fach, with half a pound of vegetables, viz. celery, onions, leeks, turnips, and carrots chopped fine, equal parts of each excepting carrots, of which there must not be more than *one small root* chopped small; sprinkle a little salt over the vegetables, and let all stew slowly with water boiling round until the roots are thoroughly done; then strain the soup off into a pan, place the roots on a dish till the next day, and the vegetables will be excellent mixed in broth for family use. The following day the soup will be a jelly, from the face of which the fat must be removed. When the soup is wanted, put the jelly into a large basin or pan over a saucepan of boiling water; when hot, taste, and add any herbs required for flavouring, or any additional vegetables, if wanted, can be put in and stirred round till sufficient flavour is obtained.

The best parts of the roots of tongue are to be cut in neat squares or mouthfuls, and put into the soup to warm before it is served. No water need be added to the roots beyond what they will imbibe in the well.

No. XXI.

TO CLARIFY FAT.

All fat which is not used fresh should be clarified in the following manner. Cut up the fat in very small pieces, and put it into a large double saucepan, which should be kept on purpose; when perfectly liquefied from the heat of the water which has been boiling round it, pour it into a very large pan holding four or five gallons of boiling water, and stir the liquid fat briskly with a stick round and round; let the whole cool, and next morning the fat will be on the surface in a white cake, which can be cut round and across with a knife and taken off in pieces; the under part of each piece should be scraped, if any impurity adheres to it; the cakes of fat can then be broken up and put into little pans, holding from one to three pounds each, which being placed in the screen before the kitchen fire, will melt again, and on being removed to a cold place will congeal, and, if wanted for keeping long (if the pans are not filled too full), a piece of linen or calico, or even paper, can be placed over the top, and a piece of wood (like a bung) can be pressed down on the fat with the cloth, or calico, under it, by which means the air is excluded, and the fat will keep for some time.

N.B.—The pan to hold the boiling water into which the fat is to be poured should also have boiling water put into it to stand for half an hour *before* the fat is ready; this *first* water being poured off, the pan will have *become hot*, and the second supply of boiling water will be scalding hot when the liquid fat is poured into it; but otherwise the cold pan would have abstracted so much heat from the boiling water that the water would no longer be hot enough for the purpose of clarifying and purifying the fat properly. The fine fat which is obtained from the boiling and stewing of beef, veal, and mutton, only requires one clarification for keeping, but *dripping* from roast meat should have *two*, and, as a general rule, fat should be kept separate according to its sort. *Dripping* should never be mixed with any other fat, and fried fat (which should have two or three clarifications) is always inferior for any other cooking purpose, and should also be kept by itself, whilst the flavoured fats from beef and veal are best for savoury cooking purposes when *un-*clarified, if used fresh, as they possess all the *aroma* of the vegetables with which the meat has been stewed.

No. XXII.

BREAD SAUCE.

Two ounces of fine bread crumbs, half a pint of milk, one small white onion whole, four black pepper-corns whole. Stew for forty minutes in double sauce-pan, stirring well; then add two tablespoonfuls of cream; stir again, and take out the onion and the peppercorns before the sauce is served.

No. XXIII.

THE HERMIT'S MARROW-BONES.

The marrow taken out of the bones weighed five ounces. The bones weighed three pounds. The bones were broken small with an iron hammer, and put into the digester with three pints of water, stewed slowly on the stove for four hours. The marrow taken off the top when cold weighed five and a half ounces, under which was one pint of fine jelly; the bones were re-broken and stewed again with two pints of water : the marrow when cold weighed one ounce and a half, and there was three-quarters of a pint of jelly. The bones were broken the third time and stewed with one pint and a half of water for three hours ; one ounce and a quarter of marrow was produced and a quarter of a pint of jelly. The marrow altogether weighed thirteen ounces and a quarter. The total of jelly was two pints. The marrow taken out of the bones before they were stewed was put into a double saucepan with a quart of cold water, and simmered till the marrow had melted. But when wanted for mince pie *meat*, it is *not* to be clarified. When *clarified*, it is for *mince pie paste*, or other pastry. (See Mince Pies, page 444.)

No. XXIV.

THE HERMIT'S SOUP FOR POOR PEOPLE.

Three pints of peas, soaked in the well all night ; then put in the double with three quarts of water, and stew five hours. Chop very small, onions, celery, leeks, turnips, and carrots, three pounds altogether ; stir in single saucepan over stove with a half pound of top fat for *ten minutes*, add one pound of oatmeal, and stir again well for five minutes more ; then put them into the double, together with twenty quarts of

broth from boiled beef (not oversalted) or bone
stock, to stew for an hour. Any pieces of dressed
meat to spare can be cut up and added at last.

No. XXV.

THE HERMIT'S SHEÉP'S-HEAD BROTH.

Two sheeps' heads, weighing five pounds and a
quarter. Put in double with a quart and three quarters
of a pint of water, two ounces of onions, three ounces of
celery, four ounces of leeks, four ounces of turnips,
three ounces of carrots, and a bunch of sweet herbs,
all chopped small, stewed slowly for five hours. Broth
produced three pints and a quarter. The meat taken
off the bones after boiling weighed one pound and a
half, and the bones two pounds. The bones were then
broken small and put into the digester with two
pints of water, stewed for five hours. Jelly produced,
one pint. The bones were then re-broken, and
stewed with one pint of water for two hours and a
half: jelly produced, three-quarters of a pint. Total
of good broth produced from two sheeps' heads, two
quarts and one pint, to which the meat was added
cut up in mouthfuls, and put in at last.

No. XXVI.

HERMITS CHICKEN BOILED IN A JUG.

Weight of chicken, three pounds; water, three quarters of a pint. Put together in a jug, the jug being placed in a saucepan of boiling water, and covered over with a saucer; boiled two hours and a half; produced one pint and a half of jelly. The meat was then excellent for eating. The bones weighed, after the meat was taken off, three quarters of a pound; broken up and stewed two hours in a digester with three pints of water, produced one pint and a half of jelly; re-broken and stewed the second time in two pints and a half of water, produced a pint and a quarter of jelly.

Total produce of Chicken.—One pint and a half of best chicken broth or jelly; two pints and three-quarters of jelly from the bones: nourishing jelly in all, two quarts and a quarter of a pint.

No. XXVII.

MINCED VEAL.

Cut (not chop) three-quarters of a pound of veal in small squares thus ▪; chop fine, onions and celery one ounce each, add a *little* thyme * and parsley; put the whole into a single saucepan, with half an ounce of fine top fat from soups (veal to be preferred); stir incessantly on a slow heat for ten minutes; add half an ounce of flour; stir five minutes more; then put the whole into a double saucepan, in which has been previously warmed half a pint of veal stock; let all stew together for a quarter of an hour; then strain through a wire sieve and return it into the double saucepan; add two tablespoonfuls of cream, stir well, and then put in the cold minced veal; stir well again, and let it remain in the double in a slow heat for half an hour before it is served.

No. XXVIII.

HARICOT OF MUTTON.

Boil twelve button onions till tender, and having cut up a neck of mutton into cutlets, put them into a single saucepan or stewpan, stir them round and round on the stove over a steady heat until browned, but not burnt, then put them into a double; take half a pint of the water in which the onions have been boiled (while quite hot) and add to the mutton cutlets,

---

* Orange Thyme.

adding also two ounces of raw onions or leeks, ditto celery cut in pieces, one ounce of turnips, and half an ounce of carrots cut small, a nosegay of orange thyme, basil, and savory, and a sprinkling of salt. Let all stew together slowly till the cutlets are tender, then pour off the gravy, and put it away where it will cool *as speedily as possible ;* leave the cutlets and vegetables in the double, taking care that the vegetables are both over them and under them, and leave them on the stove to keep warm, but not in any fierce heat, adding the boiled button onions which had been put aside, that they may *warm* while the *gravy is cooling ;* as soon as the fat can be removed from the top of the gravy, take it off, and pour the gravy back upon the cutlets and vegetables, and as soon as it is hot it is ready to serve with the gravy and button onions, which must be separated from the chopped onions or leeks. Some turnips and carrots must have been stewed till tender in another double saucepan (*previously*) in beef jelly stock to add to the above : the carrots require to be boiled for half an hour longer than the turnips.

No. XXIX.

LOBSTER SAUCE.

Take a fresh hen lobster full of spawn, put the spawn and the red coral into a mortar, add to it half an ounce of cold clarified marrow, pound it quite smooth, and rub it through a hair sieve with a wooden spoon, pull the meat of the lobster to pieces with forks, put it in a basin and pour a small quantity of vinegar over it, just enough to give it sharpness; cut one ounce of fresh butter into little bits, put it into a double with a dessert-spoonful of fine flour, mix the butter and flour together into a paste before you put it on the fire, then stir in two tablespoonfuls of milk over the stove (with the water boiling round the double); when well mixed add six tablespoonfuls of lobster jelly, stir all the same way, and when thoroughly blended, and the consistence of cream, put in the meat of the lobster to which the vinegar was added, but previously drain it well from the vinegar by laying it on a cloth for a minute or two; stir the lobster and the sauce together till the lobster is hot, and then having at hand a small empty double saucepan with boiling water, pour a small quantity of the lobster sauce into the empty double, and mix in the lobster paste made with marrow till thoroughly blended, then pour the whole back to the lobster, and after well stirring it is ready. The lobster jelly is made from the shell of the lobster, which having been previously broken small and stewed well in a very clean digester, and treated in the same way as bones, will (when cold) produce a jelly highly flavoured with lobster, which adds very much to the flavour of the sauce.

N.B.—The lobster paste made with the coral and spawn is chiefly valued on account of the scarlet colour it imparts to the sauce, and also for its taste, but its scarlet colour will be destroyed by too long exposure to great heat; it is, therefore, very desirable that it should be put in at the very last, and mixed as quickly as possible. Where fish is continually eaten, a digester should be kept solely for stewing fish-shells or bones.

No. XXX.

SHRIMP SAUCE.

Take the shells of the shrimps, pound them slightly, and stew them with a very little water in a double saucepan for two hours; the shrimp water thus made is then to be strained off, and used instead of plain water, exactly in the same manner as ordered in No. 29 for Lobster Sauce, being added to the butter, flour, and milk. When the sauce is thus made, nothing more is wanted than to put in the shrimps, and, stirring well, let them stew for about a quarter of an hour.

N.B.—The reason the Hermit did not recommend the shells of shrimps to be put into a digester, was because they are in too small a quantity to require it, and sufficient flavouring can be very well extracted in a small double saucepan.

No. XXXI.

SOUTH WALES SALMON.

As soon as a salmon is killed it ought to be crimped, by making incisions between the head and the tail, two inches wide, and one inch deep. It should then be put in cold water (well water is best) for one hour, then put it on in a fish-kettle (if too large cut it in three) with as much cold water as will cover it; one quarter of a pound of salt, and as much vinegar as will make the water slightly acid. As soon as the water is scalding hot, (but *not to boil*,) take it off and pour the water into a pan and put it away in a cold place, leaving the fish in the strainer, and placing the strainer with the fish upon it over the pan of hot fish-water to cool together, where it should remain till the next day, when the fish should be placed again *in* the fish-kettle with the same water in which it was scalded, and when it is again warmed it is done. *It must not boil.*

When there is more dressed salmon than can be eaten, it is particularly good fried in batter. It should be slightly sprinkled with salt before the batter is added, and if there is any Granville fish sauce ready, or to spare, a little of it put on the pieces of salmon under the batter is a great improvement.

No. XXXII.

PRESERVATION OF JELLY STOCKS FOR SOUPS IN SUMMER AND WINTER.

One of the numerous mistakes which are made with respect to the preservation of stocks in *summer*, is that if a basin or other vessel holding a hot liquor is put in a pan of cold water, it will not only speedily cool the stock, but that if left there it would preserve it longer; whereas the fact is, that unless the vessel containing hot liquid can be left in running water, or

have the cold water surrounding it continually changed
a hot pan or basin, with hot soup, will speedily warm
the cold water into which it is plunged, and in warm
weather it is thus *kept* in a tepid bath, and will turn
sour sooner, instead of the heat being carried off by
the outward air. Another mistake is very common
with reference to the removal of fat which congeals
on the top of stocks. In cold weather the surrounding atmosphere cools the vessel containing the broth
or stock as quickly as the fat rises and congeals upon
the surface; but in warm weather the stock remains
warm underneath the congealed fat, and therefore if
the fat is not speedily removed after it is cold, there
is great danger of the stock speedily turning sour
underneath from being kept for a length of time in a
pan which remains warm without any air on the surface; but in cold weather, when the pan is cold, and
surrounded by a cold atmosphere, and the stock has
from that cause become a cold jelly, there is no
danger of the above result; but, on the contrary, the
fat being allowed to remain on the top keeps the air
from the jelly and tends to its preservation; notwithstanding this a good manager will always have the
stocks scalded frequently, by placing the pan over a
saucepan of boiling water, taking care to break up
the jelly by stirring it up with a wooden spoon from

the bottom, by which means the heat sooner pene-
trates, and there is less danger of a careless cookmaid
removing the pan before the liquor is thoroughly
heated through, in which case it is certain to turn
sour.

No. XXXIII.

WELSH MUTTON CHOPS.

Cut the chops off the neck of Welsh mutton; do
not remove the fat, and trim as little as possible; broil
on a gridiron over a sharp fire; sprinkle with a little
pepper and salt; take care not to scorch or to let the
gravy fall upon the hot stove; serve in a very hot
dish with their own unadulterated gravy; do not add
butter or any made sauces: about ten minutes will
finish them. The Hermit considered that mutton
chops never were so good as when served between
two hot plates separately to each person. Mutton
chops cut from a neck or loin, and fried in batter the
moment they are taken off the gridiron, make an
excellent dish. They should be fried in top fat from
veal or beef soups. The batter is one tablespoonful
of flour mixed with as much milk as will make it a
smooth paste; add one egg beaten up; dip the chops
hot into the batter, and fry for about five minutes in

a stewpan: a little salt may be added to the batter
if liked, and chopped vegetables, but they are not
necessary.

No. XXXIV.

BOILED EGGS.

Eggs only require to be put into cold water, whatever their size may be, and when the water boils the
eggs are done.

No. XXXV.

BAKED APPLE DUMPLINGS.

Peel and core the apples; then make a thin paste
with two ounces of flour and one ounce of fresh
butter; rub the butter through the flour, then wet
the paste with a quarter of a pint of milk, in which
the yolk and white of an egg has been beaten up;
when well blended, roll the paste out and cut it into
squares; put one apple in the centre of every square
of paste, and fill the hollow out of which the core
was taken with sugar; wrap the paste neatly round
the apple, so as to be quite round. Glaze with white
of egg and a little white powdered sugar, and bake in
a slow oven for half an hour.

No. XXXVI.

GRANVILLE FISH SAUCE.

One small anchovy well pounded in a mortar, one shallot chopped fine, two tablespoonfuls of sherry, half a tablespoonful of best vinegar, six whole black peppercorns, a little nutmeg, and a very little mace. Simmer the above ingredients altogether in a double saucepan, stirring well all the time, until the shallot is soft; then take an ounce of butter in another double saucepan, with as much flour as will make it into a stiff paste; add the other ingredients which have been stewing, and stir it well till scalding hot for about two minutes, then add six tablespoonfuls of cream: stir well, and strain. This sauce was considered by the Hermit to be a difficult and complicated recipe to execute.* The only written recipe he possessed was old, very vague, and unsatisfactory; but, nevertheless, the sauce was made in perfection under his directions, and the traveller wrote down as well as he could what he saw executed, and was informed that when properly made it was even better the second day than the first, and only required to be warmed over a saucepan of hot water. It is suitable for salmon and every other sort of fish; but the Hermit drew his attention to the impossibility of any one making it either good or twice alike who was deficient in the organ of taste; as if the anchovy or shallot was larger or smaller, or the butter not the very freshest and best, or if there was too much or too little nutmeg and mace, or if the cream was of a different consistency, the flavour would be altered, and the greatest discretion is necessary in using mace, which, if overdone, the whole is spoiled. The written recipe belonged to the Hermit's family papers, but his mother understood how it ought to be made, and had personally taught the grandmother of Gwenllian.

No. XXXVII.

MEAGRE SOUP.

Chop fine three turnips, four potatoes, four onions, one carrot and lettuce, four ounces of bread crumbs: put into a single stewpan with four ounces of top fat; stir briskly ten minutes over a hot stove; then add a spoonful or two of flour, sufficient to make it into a stiff pulp; then add two quarts of bone stock,*

---

* Roman Catholics cannot have the slightest objection to the Hermit's bone stock, which is made from bare bones of

and after stirring well all together, pour into a double
saucepan, and let it stew slowly for three quarters of
an hour; then add a pint of boiling milk, stir well,
and pass through a wire sieve; return it into the
double; add any seasoning required of salt or herbs,
&c., and it is ready to serve: it can be eaten with
fried bread like pea-soup, or larger pieces fried and
put into the soup at the last.

No. XXXVIII.

TO SALT BEEF.

Round of beef weighing fifty pounds; divide it as
evenly as possible through the whole length.   Lay it
with the skin undermost and the fleshy part upper-
most; cut gashes across the thickest part from one end
to the other, taking care not to cut it through.   Cut
off all the ragged pieces, and *reduce* the thickness of
the inside flesh *where necessary*, so that it may be

---

cooked meat, after every shred of meat has been taken from
them, and is perfectly tasteless, but is a much lighter and more
wholesome medium than the quantities of butter with which it
is customary to make meagre soups.   The one is *as much* an
animal product as the other.   Fat is always allowed instead of
butter, and is much more wholesome in all savoury cookery,
when treated in the manner practised in the cell of the Hermit.

filleted in a good shape, to secure which object a person salting must roll it round to try what the shape will be, and trim it until it will make a firm and compact round; take out all sinews and slimy particles, and wipe the meat thoroughly dry with a clean cloth, carefully cutting out the kernels; also trim the end of the flap, and cut it into a tapering shape. Have a pound of finely-pounded salt ready in the oven or hot closet, and sprinkle the warm salt into all the gashes and interstices of the meat; then rub in the whole of the remainder of the salt with the hand until the meat has acquired a greyish-blue tint, and there is no place left of a bloody red colour; bestow half a pound upon each half-round in this manner, and then putting them full length, with the skinny side next the stone, leave them to drain into a pan, which is to be placed conveniently to receive the brine below the salting table; rub another quarter of a pound of hot salt into each round the same night, ditto the following morning, ditto the following evening, do the same on the third morning, by which time each half-round will have had a pound and a half of hot salt rubbed into it. On the third afternoon place both the half-rounds in a large pan with a sufficient quantity of brine to cover them, composed of a gallon of cold water to a pound of

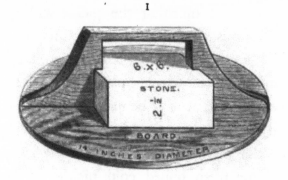

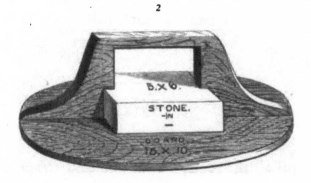

No. 1. Wooden Board and Handle, with a square Stone fixed in the centre for Weight, to keep Salt Beef and Pork under the · Pickle.

salt; turn them about well in the brine the same evening; the next morning the pickle will be quite bloody, and must be thrown away; then cover the rounds with a cold boiled pickle of the same strength, the salt and water of which must be boiled the previous evening that it may be *quite cold* and ready for use; turn the rounds every night and morning, and whenever the pickle is muddy or bloody it must be exchanged for fresh boiled cold pickle of the same strength. Boil the beef at the end of five or six days. If you wish to have the liquor of use for the poor, and the beef not oversalted for eating, it is always better to have a pan for each half-round if it can be managed, as they are easier to turn and better attended to.

No. XXXIX.

TONGUES TO SALT.

Cut off all the roots,* wash well and scrape clean, and rub well with hot salt night and morning for two days, until they are no longer slimy; especially rub the salt well into the parts where the roots have been cut off; then put the tongues into a pan and cover with pickle made as follows:—Three quarts of water, one pound and three-quarters of common salt, quarter of a pound of saltpetre, quarter of a pound of bay salt, quarter of a pound of brown sugar, an ounce of black peppercorns, a little thyme;* boil well all together, and put to cool, and when cold cover the tongues. They are ready for use in a fortnight to three weeks; the time differs according to the size and age of the tongues, but a little experience will soon teach a cookmaid by the touch when they are sufficiently hardened. If from any circumstances they are left in pickle until they are too salt, the evil can be remedied by soaking in spring water before they are boiled, and if very much oversalted, the water in which they are boiled should be poured off when they are scalding hot, and fresh boiling water put in to finish cooking them.

No. XL.

FRESH PORK TO DRESS.

Pork for pies should be deprived of all superfluous lard, and then stewed in a double in a quarter of a pint of water to the pound of meat, a little onion and

---

* The above recipe was given to the Author by Mr. Howell (man-cook), 68, Park Street, Grosvenor Square, and has been often tested.

celery cut small, and a little salt, till the meat is tender. The gravy should then be strained off and the meat put aside; the pieces of onion and celery can be picked out. The next day, the cold fat being removed from the surface of the gravy, it will be found a finely-flavoured and delicate savoury jelly. The pork meat can then be cut into proper-sized mouthfuls if for large pies; superfluous fat, bone, or sinews being taken off, and a sufficient quantity of the jelly put into the baking dish for gravy. If properly done there will always be more than sufficient, and the overplus can be used to fill up the pie after it is baked, as directed for mutton pie (see page 395), and is very good for soups.

For roast pork always take off the rind, leaving only as much lard adhering to the meat as can be eaten with it; *scotch* it across and across, and sprinkle with sage and onion very finely chopped; baste well; it will soon brown outside, and when brown take it down, put it into a double, and put the greater part of the gravy with it, reserving only enough to dish it with, which put aside; put half a quarter of a pint of boiling water in the double to every pound of pork, and, keeping water boiling round it, finish it off in the double. The gravy that has been put aside after the cold fat has been removed from the top is to be re-warmed and dished with it. Pork can of course be roasted entirely before the fire, but the advantage of cooking it in the above manner is, that it yields a great deal of extra gravy, which, when deprived of the fat, is excellent for family pea-soup.

Pork sausages are preferred by the Hermit when made of the meat of pork previously dressed in a double, or the remains of pork pies, the meat to be pounded in a mortar, as directed in No. XVI. If pepper is desired for pork pies or sausages, it should be added at the last, as pepper would spoil all the overplus pork jelly stock for soups.

No XLI.

HAMS TO CURE.

Beat or roll the ham well with a rolling-pin on the fleshy side, rub in one ounce of saltpetre and three ounces of salt, well mixed, finely powdered, and warm; take one pound of pounded common salt, and one pound of treacle, mix together and make thoroughly hot in a double saucepan, then rub into the ham well by degrees (one spoonful at a time) till the whole is absorbed—it will take an hour to do it properly; let it lie one night, the next day rub in half a pound more of common salt pounded fine, rub it in evenly all over the ham, let it lie till brine runs from it; then turn the ham in its own pickle, and rub it well every day till it begins to shrink, and it may then be hung up in an airy place and dried very gradually. Three weeks or a month is the ordinary time to cure a ham.

N.B.—After the first rubbing with saltpetre the ham must be placed in a long pan, out of which it can be taken, and put upon the stone to rub in the treacle and salt, but it must be kept in the pan or the pickle will be lost. Hams cured in this way, as in all others, should be used before they are old and rusty, but when used in the above manner they are particularly good dressed very fresh, and small hams from porkers should be cured in this way when required for eating cold.

No. XLII.

BRAWN.

Soak a fresh pig's head in cold salt and water—one pound of salt to a gallon of water—for twelve hours, changing when bloody; then boil in a double till tender with as much water as will cover it; chop small, sprinkle pepper and salt between each layer of the chopped pig's head until the brawn tin, or mould, is filled, then put on the wooden lid which fits within the mould, but rises above it, and place a weight upon it; the next day it can be turned out. It must be kept in a bran pickle if not eaten immediately.

Pigs' ears and pettitoes can be done in the same way, and added to the pig's head, unless wanted otherwise. The jelly from boiling the brawn (if it has not been too much salted) is a good addition to soup for the poor.

PICKLE FOR BRAWN.

Take as much water as will more than cover the brawn in a pan, mix in as much bran as will thicken it, add salt *in the proportion* of one pound to a gallon; simmer altogether in a double for two hours; strain it, and pour it off to cool. When cold, pour it off gently into another pan, keeping back the sediment; then add in the proportion of one quart of vinegar to the gallon, and then pour over the brawn.

No. XLIII.

TAPIOCA PUDDING FOR CHILDREN OR INVALIDS.

Tapioca two ounces; put in a double with one pint of milk, sugar to taste, and a bit of lemon-peel;

when the tapioca is thoroughly soft and blended with the milk, put it to cool on a flat dish ; when cold put it into a basin, and mix in one egg beaten up, white and yolk together ; it must be well stirred in through the tapioca to be thoroughly blended; bake with water in the baking-tin, so that the bottom of the pudding may not be burnt before the top is done.

RICE PUDDING.

Rice, one ounce and a half, put in a double with a pint and a half of milk ; sweeten to taste. Let it stew till thoroughly soft; flavour with lemon-peel if liked ; put upon a flat dish to cool; when cold beat up one egg, yolk and white, and mix thoroughly through it; bake with water in the baking-tin, for reasons above given.

RICE PUDDING WITHOUT EGGS.

Two tablespoonfuls of rice, two teaspoonfuls of white sugar, one pint and a half of skim or new milk ; put altogether in a baking-dish, fill the baking-tin with cold water, and put in a steady slow oven for two hours; if the oven is very slow, it will take three hours.

No. XLIV.

CIL GOVER BISCUITS.

Two pounds of flour, half a pint of milk, and half a pint of water; knead well, and roll and beat hard for half an hour with the rolling-pin till the paste is so stiff it will crack; cut out the biscuits of the size marked below, and about a quarter of an inch thick, prick them, and bake in a quick oven.

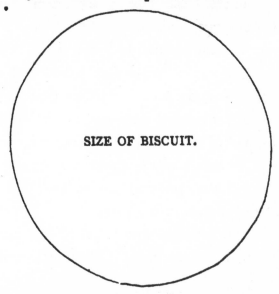

SIZE OF BISCUIT.

N.B.—A great deal depends on the heat of the oven; it must be *as sharp as possible without burning*. The biscuits when properly done are slightly browned, or mottled, in patches over the surface. These biscuits are particularly wholesome for invalids and children. The Hermit's patients often recovered upon them when they could not eat any bread; and in fevers these biscuits broken in small bits, and soaked in cold water from the spring, frequently agree when no other nourishment can be taken.

No. XLV.
THE HERMIT'S ROCK CAKES.

Four ounces fresh butter, six ounces fine sugar, six yolks of eggs, and one pound of flour; beat the butter to a cream, then add the eggs, the sugar, and the flour; mix into a stiff paste, and add four whites of eggs and beat all together well for a whole hour; add previously caraway seeds, or currants well plumped to the flour. Drop the mixture on the baking-tin in rough pieces about the size of a large walnut and the shape of little rocks. Bake in a quick oven for twenty minutes.

N.B.—Two persons are required to beat these cakes by turns for an hour. They keep well in tin boxes.

No. XLVI.

THE HERMIT'S RICE BREAD.

Six pounds of flour and one pound boiled cold rice well mixed through the flour; then add a quarter of a pint of barm, leave it to rise for half an hour, then knead it with the water in which the rice was boiled, and in half an hour it is ready for baking, if the barm is good. Bake for an hour in a moderate oven.

RICE BREAD (ANOTHER SORT).

Boil a quarter of a pound of rice till quite soft, put it on a sieve to drain, when cold mix it well with three-quarters of a pound of flour and a spoonful of barm; let it stand for three hours to rise, then knead it up, and roll it in about a handful of flour so as to make it dry enough to put in the oven; about an hour and a quarter will bake it. It should not be cut till a day or two old, and then looks like a honey-comb.

No. XLVII.
FOR ST. VITUS'S DANCE.

Take as much mistletoe (that which grows on the whitethorn) and moss from the bark of the ash-tree as three quarts of water will cover, boil them till they are reduced to three pints; strain it, and, when cold, take a teacupful three times a day.

N.B.—This prescription actually cured a Welsh boy when all other means had failed.

No. XLVIII.
BEES' FOOD.

One teacupful of treacle and two of water. Simmer it for half an hour with a little salt in a jug plunged in a saucepan of boiling water; keep in a cool place, and tie the jug over with paper; feed the bees by pouring a little every night into a wooden scoop, which put into the hole of the hive, and take out the first thing in the morning.

PASTE FOR APPLE OR OTHER TARTS. *

Take four ounces of fine flour on the board, rub one ounce of fresh butter through the flour, mix the yolk of one egg smooth in a quarter of a pint of skim milk, wet the flour with the mixture to a proper temper, roll it out, then line the edge of two tart dishes, put in the fruit and cover with the paste, which will be sufficient for two tarts; the white of the egg is to be beat with a fork upon a plate till it is in small bubbles, then put it evenly all over the top paste of the tarts with a feather, put the tarts in the baking-tin into which cold water has previously been poured, place them in the oven for a few minutes until the egg froth is sufficiently set to be sugared,

---

* The *un*numbered recipes are those which are not referred to in Hermit's lessons.

take them out, strew sugar over them quickly, and replace them in the oven till baked sufficiently.

N.B.—Practical experience alone can teach the proper heat of the oven; it is not absolutely necessary to put them in the oven before they are sugared, but some persons succeed better in making the rough glaze by doing so; others produce exactly the same effect by sugaring the white of egg as soon as it is put on, before the tart is placed in the oven.

QUINCES FOR ADDITION TO APPLE TARTS.

Cut the quinces in quarters. To five pounds of fruit put three pounds of sugar and half a quarter of a pint of water; put them in pint jars; put plates or saucers over the jars, and let them simmer very gently for three hours placed in boiling water; put the peels in with them, and take them out when done; the overplus of syrup may be bottled, and also used to flavour tarts. It will prevent waste of sugar, if the peels are stewed the first hour without sugar, then take out the peels and add the sugar, and simmer for two hours longer.

TO DRY HERBS.

Cut the herbs on a dry day just before they flower; cut off the hard parts of the stems, and dry the tender tops and leaves in an oven (or hot closet or screen) between two dishes, as quickly as possible, provided they are not burnt; pick off the leaves while hot, pound them well in a mortar, and put them into well-stoppered bottles; they ought to be *green* but crisp. The best time for drying herbs is when they are in bud.*

BASIL is in the best state for drying from the middle of August and three weeks after.

KNOTTED MARJORAM, from the beginning of July and during the same.

WINTER SAVORY, the latter end of July and throughout August.

SUMMER SAVORY, the latter end of July and throughout August.

THYME, LEMON-THYME, ORANGE-THYME, during June and July.

MINT, latter end of June and during July.

SAGE, August and September.

TARRAGON, June, July, and August.

CHERVIL, May, June, and July.

---

* All good managers should keep this calendar by them, and take care to gather their herbs when in bud (not blossom); and those who have a gardener should give him a duplicate list, that the herbs may not be sent in for winter preservation when past their prime.

BURNET and BASIL, June, July, and August.

PARSLEY, May, June, and July.

FENNEL, May, June, and July.

ELDER FLOWERS, May, June, and July.

RASPBERRY VINEGAR.

Bruise eight pounds of raspberries and pour on them three pints of good gooseberry or sugar vinegar, let them stand *twenty-four* hours, frequently stirring them with a wooden spoon; put six pounds of loaf-sugar, broken in large lumps, into an earthen vessel, and the fruit and vinegar into a jelly-bag, wrung out in boiling water; let it drop upon the sugar till the juice is drained out, pressing it gently now and then; pour the liquor into a preserving-pan, and let it simmer until it boils up slowly over a moderate fire, and when cold bottle it. When wanted for use, put one or two spoonfuls in a tumbler of spring water, and, if too sweet, add a few drops of vinegar when drunk. A stone jar is the best to boil it in, set in a vessel of boiling water.

DUCHESS OF BEDFORD'S TEA-CAKES.

Take two pounds of fine flour, three ounces of pounded sugar, four ounces fresh butter, four eggs well beaten, one large tablespoonful, or half an ounce, of barm (or German yeast), one pint of new milk; melt the butter in the milk, which must be warmed, mix all together and beat it well; let it stand one hour, then put it in well-buttered small round tins; let them be *well proved*. Bake in a quick oven twenty minutes.

_____

RHUBARB JAM.*

Boil an equal quantity of rhubarb cut up, and gooseberries before they are *quite ripe*, with three-quarters of a pound of crystallized moist sugar to one pound of fruit. When boiled, it will make an excellent jam, similar to apricot.

It will keep some time in a cool dry place, tied down as usual.

_____

APPLE BREAD.

Boil twelve apples till soft; core and peel them, break them up, and pulp through a sieve; put sugar to taste, and mix them with twice its weight of dough, and bake them in a very slow oven.

---

* This receipt was given to the Hermit by the venerable Mrs. Faulkener, of Tenby, South Wales, aged ninety-three, for many years landlady of the principal hotel there (*then* the White Lion).

THE HERMIT'S MINCE-PIES.

Squeeze the juice out of three large lemons, boil the rind (till a straw will go through) in several waters to extract the bitterness; chop them fine, add half a pound of sweet almonds pounded fine, one pound of currants, one pound lump sugar, one pound raw marrow, cinnamon, nutmeg, and a *very little* mace; mix it up to a proper consistency. The currants must be very well cleaned and plumped by pouring boiling water on them, and drying in dry cloths before the fire, and picking them well. To be baked in very small tin pattipans, the paste being made with clarified marrow, *not butter*.

A COMPLICATED VEAL PIE, BUT VERY GOOD, TO BE EATEN COLD.

Quarter of a pound of suet, quarter pound bread crumbs, a tablespoonful of parsley leaves chopped fine, a small quantity of tarragon and basil chopped fine, half a tablespoonful of lemon thyme, ditto sweet marjoram chopped fine and eschalot, all to be chopped fine, and pounded, also one tablespoonful and a half of rind of lemon, cut as thin as possible, and pounded with a lump of sugar that has been well rubbed on the lemon before the peel has been cut off, chop and

pound a small quantity of lean dressed ham or tongue.
Bake raw lean veal in a Ffwrn fach with one-quarter
of a pint of water to the pound, and put pure fat
over it (its own is the best) in a very slow oven, or
stew it in a double saucepan. After it is done pour
off the gravy, which will become jelly, cut in very
small pieces, and pound it in a mortar with all the
above ingredients moistened with the veal-jelly; and
after all are thoroughly mixed and pounded together,
beat up the yolk and white of an egg, mix it with all
the pounded ingredients, then beat it all well together
again. Put a layer of very thin boiled cold ham at
the bottom of the dish, then add the forcemeat till
the dish is full.

It must be moistened with the jelly stock which came
from the veal. The dish is to be first lined with puff
paste, and carefully baked with water in the baking-
tin, well soaked through in the oven, and yet not dried
or burned. When cold, to be turned upside down.

THE WELSH HERMIT'S FAVOURITE CHICKEN AND LEEK PIE.

Boil a chicken as directed in No. I., cut it up into
tidy pieces, not too large, flavour the chicken jelly
which it will have produced with a little salt and
celery, onion, and various herbs to taste; scald some

small leeks by pouring boiling water upon them, then
split them, and cut them in pieces about an inch long;
lay the pieces of chicken in the pie-dish with slices of
cold boiled tongue, the pieces of scalded leeks, fine-
chopped parsley, and the chicken jelly flavoured as
above described. The paste to be the same as ordered
for mutton-pie, No. VII. Fill the baking-tin with water;
when the paste is done take off the top ornament, and
with a jug pour in through the hole in which it was
placed three tablespoonfuls of fresh cream· previously
heated, by placing the jug containing it in a saucepan
of boiling water; replace the ornament, and serve.

N.B.—Mutton, beef, and veal make excellent pies
prepared in the above manner; but the veal also
requires tongue or ham intermingled with it, and a
very little pepper as well as salt may by some persons
be considered an improvement to mutton and beef,
though the former is not necessary, and it is more
wholesome without spice.

THE HERMIT'S MUTTON STEW.

Necks and scrags of mutton, eight pounds, cut up,
celery, half a pound, chopped small; onions, half a
pound, chopped small; water, two quarts. Stew in
the double three hours. It will produce two quarts

and one pint of good broth. Next day, cut off all superfluous fat and bare bones; put the meat on again in a double, with as much of the clear broth as is sufficient to moisten the stew, with half a pound more raw chopped onions and four pounds potatoes which have been boiled and cut up; all the fat must be previously removed from the broth when cold. The whole to stew together for one hour.

N.B.—There is always more broth produced than is required for the stew, and the overplus can be kept for use as clear, pure mutton broth, as the stronger flavour required for the stew is obtained by the chopped onions added with the potatoes, and any overplus of the sauce which is to spare when the stew is dished will resemble, potato soup, and is an excellent addition to other thickened soups.

———

ROAST HARE.

Hares in general when roasted have black heads, ears burnt to tinder, and the top of the shoulders, and very often the whole body, scorched and dried up. The proper way to roast a hare is first of all to soak it in several waters for an hour and a half (and having got rid of all the blood from the neck by cutting the neck-string, and pouring warm water over the incision to effect the above purpose) ; the hare must then be well dried, and a piece of paper saturated with liquid fat put all over the head and neck, under which there must be as much pure fat as can be tied on under the paper. Lay slices of cold boiled pork or bacon all over the back, which should also be covered with oiled paper for the first three quarters of an hour. The paper can afterwards be taken off, and the bacon also, when nearly done, to finish the roasting ; brown it and froth it. The hare must *also* be continually well basted. The art in roasting a hare is to prevent its being dry, and yet to have it brown and well frothed at the last ; it will take *from* one to two hours according to the size ; it should be tied upon a spit with skewers and roasted horizontally. Spits should never be put *through* anything that can possibly be avoided.

The meat remaining from roast hare should be hashed in the jelly made from its bones, *treated* exactly in the same manner as directed for other bones. They will make more jelly than required for hashing the meat. If the hash *is* not all eaten, it will make excellent hare soup with the overplus of the jelly. If more stock is required, the jelly from the bones of other game *or* poultry can be used also, and the whole flavoured with herbs and vegetables as required, the remainder of the hash to be added half an hour before it is wanted.*

_____

HARE STUFFING.

Two ounces of beef suet chopped fine, three ounces of fine bread crumbs, half an ounce of parsley, marjoram, winter savory and grated lemon-peel, half an ounce of shallot, nutmeg, pepper, and salt. Mix with the white and yolk of an egg. If not stiff, it is good for nothing; put it in the hare, and sew it up.

_____

GOOSE OR DUCK STUFFING.

Two ounces of scalded onion, one ounce of green sage leaves, four ounces of bread crumbs, yolk and white of an egg, pepper and salt, and some minced apple. The flavour is much milder if the onions are scalded previously.

_____

VEAL CUTLETS.

Veal cutlets should be half an inch thick, cut round and flattened; the trimmings which come off the veal (by cutting them round) should be put into a double saucepan with two or three spoonfuls of water,

_____

* Three pounds of hare bones will make three pints of hare jelly.

and finely-chopped leek roots, orange thyme, and marjory, and a small piece of lemon-peel. Stew them slowly two hours, and then strain off; while the gravy is being made the raw cutlets should have a few drops of lemon-juice squeezed upon them on a dish, and some chopped sweet herbs sprinkled over them; take all the fat off the veal gravy as soon as cold; chop very fine two ounces of leek roots, one ounce of celery, and a quarter of half an ounce of carrot, and stir in a single saucepan over the fire, with the fat obtained from the veal gravy; if any additional fat is wanted, let it be taken from veal stock or chicken stock. Stir the vegetables and fat together briskly for ten minutes, then add as much flour as will make it into a soft paste, and stir five minutes more; then add the whole mass to the veal gravy, which should be ready heated in another double sauce-pan, and, when it has simmered for three quarters of an hour, add two tablespoonfuls of cream ten minutes before it is strained; return the sauce, without the vegetables, into the double saucepan, and it is ready to dish with the cutlets; but if any additional flavour is wanted it can be previously added. The cutlets are to be rolled in egg and bread crumbs, and fried, in the same way as fish, in clarified top fat. The veal trimmings, after the gravy has been made, will be useful to make sausages, after being pounded in the mortar with a little veal jelly, and a little boiled ham or tongue, and flavoured with sage.

WELSH LEEK BROTH OR SOUP.

Blanch five or six fine winter leeks by putting them for five minutes in boiling water, after cutting off part of the head, leaving some of the green leaves attached to the roots; having split each leek in half lengthways, and cutting one half in three or four pieces, then add them to a fowl trussed for boiling, with half a pint of water to the pound weight, in a double stewpan, adding a little celery chopped small, and herbs and salt to taste. Let the water boil slowly round in the outer vessel until the chicken is tender and nearly fit to eat, then put in two dozen French plums whole; draw the saucepan aside to keep hot, but not to overboil the fowl. In about half an hour the plums will be plump and fit to eat, before which time take out the fowl, cut it into neat pieces, removing the bones, and put the pieces into the tureen, pouring the leek broth or soup over them, the leeks being then partly in pulp. If too thick, some additional veal or chicken jelly can be added to it. The plums are eaten with the meat and vegetables.

SHOULDER OF VEAL BOILED.

The jelly stock from veal boiled in the following manner was the usual foundation for the Hermit's white soups.

Shoulder weighing ten pounds, celery half a pound chopped fine, onions half a pound chopped fine, water one quart and half a pint; stewed in double till the meat is fit for eating.

It produced one quart and a pint and a half of stock, which when cold was a firm jelly.

The next day the shoulder being *re*-warmed in a double in its own stock (which is improved thereby), can be served with the following sauce:—Milk, one pint; water, one quarter of a pint; one pint and a quarter of bone stock; half a pound of rice; suet or veal's top fat, two ounces. Stir well, and stew in double three hours and a half, with four ounces of pounded ham or cold boiled pork, or else salt to taste, with finely-chopped onion: five minutes before it is served put in two or three ounces of fresh chopped parsley, and again stir well. The above sauce is not only a palatable accompaniment with veal, but an excellent foundation for a family white soup afterwards. Fried bacon or sausages can be served as accompaniments.

N.B.—The *cruel* practice of bleeding calves before they are killed, to make the meat unnaturally white, destroys the flavour of veal, and renders a meat which is not light of digestion really unwholesome.*

GLAZE OF COW'S-HEEL.

Scald a fresh cow's-heel to get the hair off; then, after well scraping, crack it across in several places, and chop up and put it in a digester with four quarts of water, and stew till it is reduced to two quarts; then pour into a pan till the next day. Then take all the oil off the top, and bottle it for the use of the stables. (This is pure neat's-foot oil.) The jelly under it will be hard, and is the material to make glaze, which is coloured by stirring quickly over the fire till it becomes a fine yellow bronze, and is thick enough to adhere to the spoon. There is less waste if coloured with a little burned sugar, as it requires less boiling down for colouring.

N.B.—The cow-heel bones ought to be done a second and third time; *re*-broken with fresh water in digester; and will make stock each time. Second time, put two quarts of water and reduce to one

---

* This cruel practice is not followed abroad, which is the reason that veal often agrees there with those who cannot eat it in England.

quart; third time, one full quart, and reduce to one pint.

It it much less wasteful to procure a cow's-heel for glaze than to allow glaze to be made of trimmings of meat, &c. &c. Glaze is *only* for *orna-ment* to *varnish* meat. It is not supposed to be eaten, but, *if* it is put on food, it *ought to be wholesome*. The usual custom of making glaze of what is called "*anything*," but means "everything," otherwise eatable, destroys a large quantity of food for no good purpose.

MUSHROOM CATCHUP.

Full-grown mushrooms are the best for catchup; cut them across and across stems and skins, put a layer at the bottom of an earthen pan and sprinkle with salt, and continue till you have used all the mushrooms you have ready; sprinkle moderately with salt over every layer, let them stand three hours, then pound them up in a mortar, and let them stand two days, stirring them up with wooden spoons twice every day; then pour the whole mass into jars, and to every quart add half an ounce of whole black pepper, ditto allspice; put the jars into an outside double surrounded by boiling water; let the water boil slowly and steadily round them two hours and a half, then take out the jars and pour the juice through a sieve into a clean double saucepan, and let the water boil around it for one hour more, then pour it into a jug or basin, and let it stand in a cold place till the next day, when very gently pour it off into half or quarter-pint bottles which have been rinsed out with spirits of wine; cork close, and cement. If it is ill-corked and not kept dry, it will spoil. The pepper-corns and allspice should be bottled with it, and the strainings can be made use of for hashes, &c. &c., if not kept longer than two or three days. The sub-stance of the mushrooms which is left behind after straining, should be pressed down flat on a plate covered over with another plate, and dried in a hot closet, or in a screen before the fire. When dry, pound and put in bottles, and use in the same way as catchup, where mushroom flavour is desired.

N.B.—Mushroom catchup is generally made with *putrefied* mushrooms, and, even when mushrooms are fresh, it is customary to keep them so long in a pan mashed, or unmashed, that they are unfit for use, the best flavour being gone and the mushrooms in a very unwholesome state. The mushrooms should be as freshly gathered as possible for catchup, and should never be kept longer than is recommended in the above recipe.

THE HERMIT'S BREAD AND BUTTER PUDDING.

Cut rice bread (see page 437) of two days old in thin slices, without crust, butter thinly with cold butter, fit them into the tart-dish you intend to use, then take them out and pour three-quarters of an inch of rather thick batter (flavoured with sugar and lemon-peel) into the bottom of the dish. Put the dish into the oven for three or four minutes to consolidate the batter, then take it out and lay a layer of slices on the batter, then pour out of a jug a sufficiency of *thinner* batter (similarly flavoured) to moisten the bread, then sprinkle a layer of currants well plumped, then another layer of slices of bread, pouring in batter in the same manner over each layer until the dish is filled to within half a quarter of an inch of the top; then make your batter thicker, so as to be of the same consistence as the first layer in the bottom of the dish, and with this (*thicker*) batter fill the dish evenly to the edge, and bake with water in the tin. If properly made it will be firm and yet light, the batter at the bottom will keep the bread from drying up with too fierce a heat, the thicker batter on the top ought to *cover* the upper layer of currants, and prevent that common but very unpleasant effect of having the slices of bread at the top of the dish scorched and curled up, and covered with currants burned to a cinder. The object of having thinner batter poured between the layers of bread is to soften the bread, as otherwise the bread would not absorb the batter and be flavoured by it.

_____

WELSH CARROT PLUM PUDDING.

Half a pound of raisins, half-pound of currants, half-pound of suet chopped fine, one ounce lemon-peel, one nutmeg, two large carrots, and two tablespoonfuls of flour; mix all well together, but the carrots must be boiled and pulped previous to mixing with the other ingredients, and the whole must be boiled two hours.

_____

ANOTHER.

Half-pound of flour, quarter of a pound of suet chopped very fine, quarter-pound bread crumbs, three-quarters of a pound grated carrot, quarter of a pound of raisins stoned, quarter of a pound well-washed and plumped currants, quarter-pound brown sugar, beat up *two whole* eggs and the yolks of four in a gill of milk; grate a little nutmeg into it, and add it to the former. Boil at least one hour.

_____

FAMILY PLUM PUDDING.

Flour twenty-six pounds, suet seven pounds, raisins nine pounds, currants four pounds, sugar four and a half pounds. If not eaten the day boiled, boil **half** the time the first day and the other half the **second,** or only warm through the second time, as **over-**boiling makes the plum puddings too soft.

Cow-heel is an excellent substitute for suet **in** making plum puddings. It must be well boiled previously, and not chopped too fine.

The subjoined pudding casket,* made of tin, was

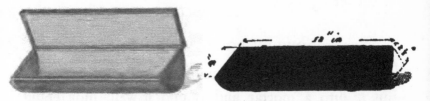

invented by the Hermit for boiling plum puddings when made in rolls to be cut in slices, the Hermit having observed that when plum puddings were boiled in cloths *only* the water became a sort of *raisin and currant soup,* and that the waste of ingredients altogether was considerable.

Each pudding turned out of these tin caskets can be divided into *ten* thick slices. The Hermit had a wooden gauge for the widows with *points* at equal distances, and each pudding was thus marked in a

---

* These Plum Pudding Caskets are to be had of Richard Jones, Tinman, Abergavenny, South Wales. Price 1s. 6d. each, or 1s. 3d. by the dozen.

moment (as soon as turned out) and cut up in the
most exact manner. A thin piece of cloth laid under
the lid after the tin is filled is all that is required, and
the lid, being shut, is tied round with strong pack-
thread passed through the loops in the lid; and when
twenty or thirty puddings are boiled at the same time
in a boiler, five or six can be tied together, and taken
out of the boiler when done with a hook by a loop
in the string.

ROWLEY POWLEY PUDDING.

Skin and chop one pound of beef suet very fine,
put it into a mortar and pound it well, moistening
with a little sweet-oil until it is the consistency of
butter.

Put one pound of flour upon your pastry slab,
make a hole in the centre, in which put a teaspoonful
of salt, and mix it with cold water into a softish
flexible paste with the right hand; dry it off a little
with flour until you have well cleared the paste from
the slab, but do not work it more than you can possibly help; let it remain two minutes on the slab,
and then lay the prepared suet on the paste; press it
out flat with the hand, then fold over the edges of
the paste so as to hide the suet, and roll it to the
thickness of half an inch; fold over one third, over

which pass the rolling-pin; fold over the other third, thus forming a square; place it with the ends before you; shake a little flour over and under, repeat the rolls and turns twice more; flour a baking sheet, lay it in a cool place for half an hour; then roll twice more, and put in a cool place for a quarter of an hour; give two more rolls (making seven in all), and it is ready for use.

Roll it out and cover with jam; tie in a loose cloth, and serve up cut in slices. This pudding may also be boiled in a bason and turned out.

BREAD PUDDING.

A pint of bread crumbs in a double saucepan with as much milk as will cover them; the peel of a lemon, a little nutmeg, and a bit of cinnamon; boil about a quarter of an hour, sweeten, take out the cinnamon and add two eggs, beat all well together. If baked, it will require half an hour; if boiled, more than an hour.

QUEEN CHARLOTTE'S ORANGE PUDDING.

Take two oranges and one lemon, grate the peel off them and mix with the juice, into which put a quarter of a pound of sugar and the yolks of five eggs; then make a little paste for the bottom of the dish. It must be baked slowly in a moderate oven, but yet be browned at the top.

APPLE SNOW.

Roast four or five apples that look white, work the pulp through a sieve; take the weight of one egg of pulp, the same of powdered sugar; beat up the apple sugar and the white of an egg together until they become as white as snow. When nearly beaten up, put in as much ground alum as will cover a sixpence, and, when quite beaten, put it very lightly piled in a dish. If liked, cream or custard can be eaten with it.

Preserved raspberries or strawberries can be used as well as apples.

LEMON CREAMS.

Rub three lemons with sugar until the aroma is absorbed, squeeze the juice of one upon the sugar, put it in a large china bowl, add a quart of cream, and whisk it continually till the froth arises; take it from the top with a spoon, and place it on a sieve; put it in the glasses a short time before it is sent to table. It will take nearly half a pound of sugar to sweeten a quart of cream with the lemon-juice.

LEMON JELLY.

Eight sheep shanks broken up and put to soak over night in cold water; then put on the fire or stove in a digester with two quarts of water, and stew until it is reduced to one; but if done in a double saucepan, one quart of water will be sufficient, and double time required, but there will not be any danger of waste. Pour off to cool, and the next day take off all the oil from the top, and what will not come off with a spoon can be wiped off with a clean soft cloth, or absorbed with soft paper. The jelly ought to be very firm, so that it would cut up in pieces: to one quart of jelly put half a pound of lump sugar broken up, the peel of one lemon and the juice of three lemons, three eggs, whites and shells; beat up together, whisk the whole over the stove till ready to boil, then draw it off sufficiently to keep it simmering slowly for a quarter of an hour, putting hot cinders or hot charcoal on the lid of the stewpan; then, having the jelly bag ready and warm, having squeezed it out in scalding water and suspended before the fire with a basin under it, pour the jelly through the jelly bag, return the first strainings back a second time into the bag till all has run through. The jelly is then finished, and may either run into a mould or be allowed to cool in a basin and cut out as wanted. Shank jelly is lighter of digestion than calves'-foot jelly, and quite as good for every other purpose.

___

TURIN STICKS.

Two pounds of white flour, two ounces of fresh butter. Rub the butter well into the flour; add two teaspoonfuls of baking powder, and sufficient pure cold spring water to mix it into a *stiff* paste; cut into little lumps of equal size, roll out into long thin sticks as quickly *as possible*; bake in rather a *quick* oven.

___

PUMPKINS.

Few vegetables are so little understood, and, consequently, so much undervalued in Great Britain, as pumpkins. Perhaps Gower, in South Wales, is the only part of the United Kingdom where pumpkins are grown as an article of diet by the rural population from their appreciation of their nutritive qualities; and there they are to be seen as on the Continent, hanging from the ceilings for winter store, in cottages and farmhouses, and any little spare corner in the field or garden is made use of to place the small mound in which to sow a few pumpkin seeds. The varieties of this plant are so numerous that it would be beyond the limit of any cookery book to attempt an enumeration of comparative merits, from the Vegetable Marrow to the Turk's Turban and the Yellow Pumpkin, which grows to such a size as to fill a wheelbarrow, but, as the Hermit was fully aware of the merits of this vegetable, it will not be out of place to note shortly from among his recipes a few of the modes in which pumpkins are available, wholesome, and nourishing in cookery. For white soup they can be used alone, with merely the addition of onion, celery, and sweet herbs for flavouring, in the same manner as the numerous vegetables mentioned in the White Soup of Gover. (See page 391.) They are excellent when boiled, sprinkled with salt and sweet herbs, and fried in egg and crumbs, like soles. Also plain, boiled in slices, and served with brown gravy. In Gower they are added to hashed meat, made into pies with apples, and put into soup. There is also a dish made by the natives which seems to evince an Eastern origin, which is made of pumpkin, mutton, and currants. Pumpkins have one peculiar quality in addition to a good deal of natural sweetness, which is, that they will absorb and retain the flavour of whatever they are cooked with; this where fruit is scarce* is a

---

* The Hermit was of opinion that the great scarcity and dearness of fruit in Great Britain, which is severely felt by the

very important characteristic, as the pumpkin is both wholesome and nourishing in itself, but, not having any flavour, its imbibing the flavour of any fruit if mixed with it is an especial advantage. If stewed with plums, it tastes exactly like them in puddings and tarts; the same with apples, rhubarb, or gooseberries and for savoury cookery it would be difficult to say in what dish it may not be used with advantage as an addition.

In America there are an endless variety of puddings of which pumpkins are the principal ingredient; and they are very easily grown. On one occasion they appeared in a field of mangel-wurzel in South Wales,

poor, arises from the *want of attention to hardy sorts of fruit* with which the climate of Great Britain will agree. In many parts of Germany, where the climate is much more severe, and where also there is a great deal of rain, there is abundance of fruit; pears, plums, and peaches, and in many places *standard apricots*. It is very true that the fruit is frequently very inferior in flavour to the fruit from English walled gardens, but it is equally good and wholesome when stewed or preserved. It is very singular that the Horticulturists of Great Britain do not pay more attention to the introduction of those kinds of fruit-trees which are hardy and bear abundantly, instead of sacrificing everything to the magnitude of specimens. *Fruit for the million* is much wanted. The purple peach (of Bonn), which is hardy and a standard, seems to be unknown in Great Britain. The pulp as well as the juice is the colour of a mulberry. (*Traveller's Note.*)

to the great surprise of the owner, as it was not in that part of the Principality where pumpkins were grown. The seeds had been accidentally mixed with those of the mangel-wurzel; they were treated in the same manner, and they came to as great perfection as if they had been grown in a garden. This sort was the large orange species, called in some places " Turk's Turban," around which there is a beautiful strip of narrow network exactly resembling nun's lace: this species is particularly sweet and hardy. There are very few kinds of gourds or pumpkins that are not edible; but some of the ornamental kinds are uneatable, or have medical properties, such as the colocynth, which so closely resembles an orange in appearance.

LOSS IN ROASTING A WELSH LEG OF MUTTON.

	s.	d.
Weight before roasting, 5¼ lbs. at 10*d.* per lb. . .	4	4½
Loss by weight of bone, 10 oz. at 10*d.* per lb. after roasting	0	6¼
Balance	3	10¼
Fat, 4 oz. at *4d.* per lb., loss at the rate of 6*d.* per lb. .	0	1½
	3	8¾

Loss in Welsh mutton, 7¾*d.* in 4*s.* 4½*d.*, or 31 in 210, nearly one-seventh ; consequently, more than half the saving in food as compared with English mutton.

LOSS IN ROASTING AN ENGLISH LEG OF MUTTON.

	s.	d.
Weight before roasting, 12 lbs. at 10*d.* per lb. . .	10	0
Loss by weight of bone, 1¾ lb. at 10*d.*	1	5½
Balance	8	6½
Fat melted away, taken from dripping-pan, 3 lbs. 2 oz. at *4d.* per lb., loss at the rate of 6*d.* per lb. . . .	1	6¾
	6	11¾

Loss in English mutton, 3*s.* 0¼*d.* in 10*s.*, or 36¼ in 120, nearly one in three ; consequently, more than double the loss in English mutton as an article of food.

The foregoing Table will show that the loss on an English leg of mutton is nearly *one* in *three*, while the loss in the Welsh leg of mutton is only *one* in *seven!* the loss being more than one-half *less* in Welsh mutton than English. It must also be remembered that in the *ordinary* manner of roasting the fat above-mentioned would either be utterly lost, or not worth above 2*d.* a pound, so that the loss in English mutton would in reality be much greater. In roasting the English leg of mutton no basting fat was needed; in the Welsh leg one-quarter of a pound was used, and one-quarter of a pound was taken from the dripping-pan afterwards. In the *ordinary* method of cooking, the bone would be a clear loss in *both* cases; but *even* the Hermit's jelly from the bone would not go very far towards repairing the loss of 3*s.* o¼*d.* in every ten shillings! And if the Hermit's process of basting and clarification of fat was not adopted, the 1*s.* 6*d.* in the above Table set down to the *credit* side must be added to the loss, or at least one-half of it. There are few greater errors than to suppose fat, large animals are either wholesome or economical.

THE HERMIT'S BAKED BEEF FOR CHRISTMAS.

Take half or whole rounds of beef, cut and prepared as described (see page 427), roll them up, and skewer them into rounds, and put each of them into the outer part of a (round) "double" (see Plate 4), which is made of iron, or galvanized iron; place on the top of the round of beef, a *star* of wood the proper size to go

within the top of the vessel, then put a stiff paste of

coarse brown flour (or flour mixed with bran) over the star to prevent any evaporation, and pour in as much water with a sprinkling of salt as will rise to about two inches, then put on the lid and bake in a brick oven; the time must, of course, depend upon the size and weight of the rounds. When done the paste at the top will look like gingerbread,* the gravy will be very strong and abundant, and the meat will be juicy and nicely browned. The gravy being poured off, and the fat taken from it when cold, it is *re*-warmed to dish up. The Hermit, when he required a number of these rounds dressed at once for a Christmas feast, used to bake them the day before, and the next day *re*-warmed them in the inner doubles in their own gravy, with hot water in the outer vessel, on a large stove. In this way they were all done punctually to the same time, equally well cooked, and an abundance of extra gravy without grease. Where a brick oven is not to be had for baking meat, the iron oven should always have *all* the fire *taken out* before the meat is put in. Meat should be baked very slowly, and be well covered in a vessel with a close-fitting lid. The ignorant practice of putting meat into open baking-tins not only entirely ruins the flavour of the meat, from the bad taste imbibed from the vapour of the fat

---

* Very useful pounded to thicken soup for the poor.

(frizzling in the iron oven), but it is very wasteful, dries up the meat, destroys the gravy, and *taints the oven* to such an extent that, if bread or cakes are baked in it afterwards before it has undergone a long and laborious purification, they would be flavoured by the same taste as pervades a house from the odour of fat frying upon hot iron.

MUSHROOMS.

Wild mushrooms are generally brought in, in larger quantities than are required for immediate consumption unless made into catchup, and, as the mushroom season is always very short, the overplus of mushrooms can be preserved for two or three days to be as good as if freshly gathered, if cooked in the following manner :—Peel the mushrooms, cut off the stems, sprinkle a little salt in the inside of the flap, and put on each flap a bit of clarified marrow about the size of a very small bean, and place them one over the other in half-pint or pint jars (the outer side down and the flap up), put the jars to stand in vessels of boiling water, and let them simmer slowly, with a bladder over the top of the jar, for an hour or two, according to the number and thickness of the mushrooms ; then put them away in a cold place. These mushrooms will be good for several days, and taste as if fresh gathered.   When used, take off the marrow, if it has congealed on the surface, and put the mushrooms on a soup-plate upon squares of toast saturated with their own gravy, which will have exuded from them in the jars, put another soup-plate on the top, and warm the whole over a saucepan of boiling water. The stems and peelings of mushrooms ought to be chopped up as soon as they are taken off, and put into small jars, with a little salt, and simmered with boiling water round them in the same manner as the mushrooms: the liquor distilled from them can be used *while fresh* for flavouring sauces and hashes.

The Hermit was very partial to mushrooms, and considered them not only wholesome for persons in ordinary health, but so nutritious that he believed them equal to meat, and questioned me closely as to the improvement of their cultivation in the present age, but I did not distinguish myself by my answers, for I really could give no account of them, excepting that rich persons had mushroom houses, where they were produced by artificial heat in the winter, and that mushroom spawn was generally purchased and was expensive, but I did *not know* whether naturalists or horticulturists had discovered any means of cultivating them in the open ground, or securing the preservation of mushrooms from one year to another in places where they spring up spontaneously, though I had often heard surprise expressed at the abundance of mushrooms in some years and the absence of them in others, in the same ground; and this being the sum and substance of my knowledge, I was taunted repeatedly, at the expense of my " *scientific friends*," who had not turned their attention to a natural production so beneficial to rich and poor, and about the natural history and cultivation of which so little (according to my report) appeared to be known; and I was advised to offer a prize for new discoveries on the subject!

GOOD FAMILY BREAD (WHITE).

Five pounds of fine bran to 28 pounds of flour.

GOOD BROWN BREAD.

Two pounds of bran to four pounds of flour.

N.B.—The brown bread, or household bread of old times, is now hardly to be met with, and is rare even in Wales, the reason being that the millers do not grind and prepare the flour in the same way as formerly, when the pure corn, having been sent to be ground, was returned by the miller with the bran and flour altogether; and in every house there was a good-wife or *widow*, who sifted the flour required for each baking, removing only the large flake bran. Bread thus made is very superior in flavour to the bread now generally used, but where the above plan cannot be followed, it is best to mix fresh sifted bran with the flour. The *flavour* of bread is in the bran, and in the absence of bran it is *flavourless*, much less wholesome, and not at all more nourishing.

WELSH PAN OR POT BREAD.

Take three pounds and a half of brown flour (flour which has only had the coarser bran taken out of it), put it to rise with about two tablespoonfuls of barm, and, when risen, mix it and knead it in the usual manner; then put it into an iron pot or a thick earthen pan, and turn it topsy-turvy on a flat stone, which should be placed on the ground in the middle of a heap of hot embers, made by burning wood, peat, or turf; cover the pot or pan entirely over with hot embers, leave it to bake, and when the ashes are cold take it out. This mode of baking produces most excellent bread, but of course it cannot be practised economically except where such rural operations are carried on as provide the necessary quantity of hot embers for other purposes within a convenient distance of the house.

OATMEAL CAKES.

Make a stiff paste with oatmeal and water or skim milk; then form it into balls with the hand about the size of small eggs; then shape with the hand round and round to the size of a small cheese-plate or large saucer; when one oat-cake is formed the right shape and thickness, turn it and shake dry oatmeal all over it; then take another, put it in the middle of the oat-cake you have made, and form that in the same manner upon the first made; when well tempered, turn it, and shake dry oatmeal all over it, and proceed in the same way until you have got eighteen oat-cakes one on the other, remembering that each must be turned, and that dry oatmeal must be put between every one, and they must be turned and *re*-turned, and shaped with the hand, until they are all of the same texture, as thin as is possible without breaking. When dry enough to put on the bake-stone (heated to the required point which practice alone can teach), bake them one at a time; have a clean cloth folded to the proper shape, and press the cake down flat on the bake-stone, where it should remain until it is of a nice light brown colour. The upper side of the cake is to be glazed before it is taken off the bake-stone; the glaze is made with egg and milk, and a little sugar is generally added, but that is only a matter of taste; some persons like a little sugar mixed with the oatmeal of which the cakes are made. As each cake is taken off the bake-stone it is laid across the rolling-pin that it may dry in a hollow shape; and as each cake becomes hard and crisp, they are again put one on the other, and are always served and kept in a pile. The rolling-pin *must not* be used in making these cakes, all must be done with the hand, and they must be flattened and worked round and round with the hand until they are almost as thin as a wafer. Great skill and dexterity, as well as practice, are necessary to make these cakes well, which when once attained, the process is very quickly executed. The *thin Welsh-oat cake* is particularly wholesome, and often agrees with invalids of weak digestion better than bread; they are sometimes eaten with cold butter or cheese, or eaten dry with milk or tea.

THICK WELSH BARLEY CAKES.

Take fine barley meal and make into a stiff dough with skim milk; roll out to the size of a small bake-stone, about three-quarters of an inch thick, and bake. It is eaten with cold butter.

THIN WELSH BARLEY CAKE.

Mix fine barley meal and milk together to the consistency of batter, and pour slowly on the bake-stone out of a jug until it has formed a circle the size of a small plate, then let it bake slowly. It ought to be very thin but soft, like a pancake or a pikelate; it is likewise eaten with cold butter.

CIL GOVER BUNS.

One pound of flour, two ounces of currants well plumped, quarter of an ounce of sugar, and a tablespoonful of barm. Melt an ounce of butter in a quarter of a pint of milk; glaze with the yolk or white of an egg. The above quantity will make twelve buns.

Mix the barm * into the flour with a little warm milk, and leave it to rise for half an hour; then knead, and let the dough rise for one hour before baking. Bake twenty minutes in a moderate oven.

TEISEN FRAU GWENT A MORGANWG.†

One pound of flour, three ounces of currants well picked and washed, a little sugar (and spice if liked); mix into a thick batter with one pint of sheep's milk-cream, butter the tin of a Dutch oven and drop it in and bake before the fire. Care must be taken in turn-

---

* *Barm* (called *Yeast* in England) is a Welsh word, although found in English dictionaries.
† Short cakes of Gwent and Morganwg.

ing; it can be cut in any shape. Cream of cows'-milk may be used, but sheep's-milk cream is best for these cakes. A variety of the Teisen Frau are made by rubbing six ounces of butter in one pound of flour and two teaspoonfuls of sugar made into a stiff dough with new milk, or sheep's-milk cream; roll it out half an inch thick, and cut to size required; bake on a bake-stone, or before the fire in a Dutch oven.

FOR HARVEST. WELSH APPLE OR RHUBARB CAKES.

Stew apples or rhubarb till soft, in a basin placed on a saucepan of boiling water. If the former, take off the peel and take out the core when done, and mash with a little brown sugar to taste. If the latter, pour off the overplus of juice for other purposes. To every five pounds of flour rub in two pounds of clarified fat, roll out the paste the size of a large baking-sheet, spread the apple or rhubarb pulp all over the square sheet of paste, then lay another thin layer of paste on the top and fasten the edges together. Bake, and when cold turn it out of the tin and cut it up in squares. Another plan of making these cakes is to form the paste the size and shape of a small cheese plate, or large breakfast saucer; put the fruit over one-half of the round and turn the other half over it, making a half-moon; then glaze and bake in a quick oven. Jam of any kind can also be used in this way for Welsh harvest cakes.

WELSH HARVEST BUNS.

One pound of flour and two ounces of clarified fat rubbed through the flour, one ounce and a half of currants, one ounce of sugar, a tablespoonful of barm (or one teaspoonful of baking powder), wet the above quantity with skim milk. It will make four very large buns or cakes.

N.B.—The two foregoing recipes were used by the Hermit for the supply of his work-people during harvest, and no people ever worked better. The cold *glâsdwfr* (one quart of milk to three quarts of cold spring water) was supplied throughout the day to men, women, and children. If the weather was hot, the milk was always scalded previously to preserve it from acidity. At four o'clock, warm tea ready mixed in jugs with sugar and milk, was taken out to every one at work, with the above harvest buns, also a piece of cheese and part of a loaf of home-made bread for those whose appetites required more than two of the above buns. At eight o'clock or earlier (if they desired it) tea was sent out again in the same manner, with bread and cheese for each person.

The apple, rhubarb, or jam cakes were used as a variety, instead of buns occasionally. It was very rarely that there was any illness during harvest among those engaged in it. Mowing commenced at three or four in the morning, and the work (when the weather was favourable) continued as long as they could see in the evening, often till past nine o'clock.

The Traveller heard it remarked, that the children employed in the Hermit's harvest always " grew fat " during that period, having good appetites and as much wholesome food as they could eat : *no fermented liquors* of *any sort or kind* were *ever given* ; the usual hour was allowed for dinner at twelve o'clock, and they supplied themselves also with breakfast as on ordinary occasions. The *glâsdwfr* when mixed in the above proportions never disagrees with the digestion ; it is cooling, refreshing, and nourishing without being heavy ; but if a larger proportion of milk was used it would disagree. In some places in Wales " *dwfr blawd ceirch* " is used instead of milk and water ; this is made by putting boiling water on oatmeal, stirring it well, and letting it stand all night, and the clear water is taken off the next day for drinking.

In noting down the above particulars, I (the

Traveller.) asked the Hermit how he avoided the introduction of intoxicating liquors in harvest time ? He replied :—" My aim has been to preserve or restore all the *good* old habits of my country, and utterly to repudiate all immoral introductions which ruin the health as well as imperil the soul. Harvest *especially* is the time when we should *do what is good*, and not *teach* and *encourage wickedness*. Many and many a man, woman, and child are taught to drink in harvest time, from the want of other sustenance than intoxicating liquors."

WELSH TOASTED CHEESE.

This celebrated national dish of Wales will appropriately conclude the present collection of recipes, which were especial favourites in the cell of the Welsh Hermit, and which, in honour of his Principality, is here given in the original language as well as in English. Welsh *toasted* cheese, and the *melted* cheese of England, called " toasted cheese," are as different in the mode of preparation as is the cheese itself ; the one being only adapted to strong digestions, and the other being so easily digested that the Hermit frequently gave it to his invalid patients when they were recovering from illness, and found that they could often take it in moderation without inconvenience when the appetite and digestion were not sufficiently restored

to take much, (if any) meat, without suffering.*—
Cut a slice of the real Welsh cheese made of sheep
and cow's milk,† toast it at the fire on both sides, but
not so much as to drop; toast a piece of bread, less
than a quarter of an inch thick, to be quite crisp, and
spread it very thinly with fresh cold butter on *one*
side (it must *not* be saturated with butter), then lay
the toasted cheese upon the bread and serve immediately on a very hot plate; the butter on the toast
can, of course, be omitted if not liked, and it is more
frequently eaten without butter.

CAWS WEDI EI BOBI.

" Torrer darn o gaws Cymreig gwneuthuredig o
laeth defaid a gwartheg, pober y ddwy ochr o flaen y
tân ond nid cymmaint ag i ddiferu; craser tafell o
fara (llai na chwarter modfedd o drwch) yn grych, a
thaener ymenyn newydd oer yn deneu iawn ar un ochr
iddo (rhaid iddo beidio cael ei lenwi o ymenyn), yna
rhodder y darn caws pobedig ar y bara, ac anfoner ef
i'r bwrdd ar ddysgl boeth yn ddiattreg. Gellir peidio

* The same observation will apply to the Welsh sheep's-
milk cheese *without toasting*, which can often be taken with
bread or biscuit and a glass of cold water, with benefit by
invalids with weak digestions.

rhoddi ymenyn ar y bara crasedig, os dewiser, ac yn amlaf bwytteir ef hebddo."

Here ends the Traveller's Book of Recipes, obtained from the Hermit of the Cell of St. Gover, though only a portion of those known and practised under the directions of the venerable recluse. The Traveller departed, as has already been mentioned, to London with his ancient but active Welsh host, regretting that he had not been able to fill another book with a list of the various wild plants yet undestroyed in that part of Wales where he had so long resided; the virtues of which were well known to the Hermit and his native countrymen, and whose Welsh names in many instances indicated either their appearance or their medical and curative properties.

The Traveller's Notebook

Letter shown by the Traveller to the Hermit from a Gentleman who wanted a Shirt.

Sir,—I beg to call your attention to the following distressing facts, for the truth of which I can vouch, having occurred to myself. For many years my respected grandmother was in the habit of presenting me with an annual stock of shirts, which she cut out and made with her own hands, my mother having died when I was an infant. I was thus happily well provided till past the age of thirty-one years, but my excellent grandmother being now defunct, and my shirts in a very dilapidated condition, I applied to the wife of a friend for the direction of any female who followed the occupation of a sempstress, as my wardrobe required renovation. I did not enter into further particulars, because experience had taught me, that although my grandmother (a gentlewoman of noble descent) no more scrupled to name the word *shirt* than to make a shirt, yet that the great improvements in education had rendered the ladies of the present generation too refined even to know that such a garment was ever worn, far less to name it. The lady to whom I applied gave me the address of a Mrs. Doolittle, residing in the next country town, about three miles distant. I inquired if there was no one nearer in any village, but I was informed there was not, and I accordingly sent for Mrs. Doolittle. When she arrived, I mentioned that I required a set of shirts, and that I would give a pattern which did not require alteration. I was rather surprised by the look I received from the very important-looking personage who had answered my summons, as she neither assented nor dissented, but stood staring, as if she had heard something alarming or insulting. I repeated

in other words what I before said, and added,
" You *understand*, I require a set of new shirts.
You have been recommended to me, and here
is the pattern. I wish you to purchase the
linen for me, and to make the shirts as quickly
as you can." Upon this, she drew up with an
air of inexpressible scorn, saying, " I think, sir,
there must be some great mistake somewhere ;
I never made such a thing in my life, sir, and
never professed to do so." " Why, are you
not a sempstress ? or what do you call your-
self ? " " I go out occasionally to assist in
trimming, and also take the higher branches
at home." " Well," rejoined I, " I thought
people who did needlework were called *sempstresses*." " I do not understand that name,
sir ; I *never heard it before* ; I was educated
in a *very superior* manner, sir." I here recollected having heard my good grandmother
say, that " the test of a needlewoman was
making a shirt," and that any one who could
make a fine shirt properly, was mistress of
plain needlework.* I therefore ventured to

---

* If *button-holes* were included.

observe, that I had always understood that
"shirt-making was *the* 'highest branch' of
needlework;" upon which Mrs. Doolittle replied, with a contemptuous gesture, that " *that*
must have been very long ago, before she was
born, as her *governess*, who taught all the modern
branches of a first-rate education, never allowed
such a garment to be mentioned in her presence." By this time I had come to the
conclusion that the longer this elegant pro-
fessor of the " higher branches " remained in
my presence, the worse the opinion we should
form of each other! I therefore speedily
wished her good morning, and applied to
another lady to recommend somebody who
would not be above undertaking the task of
renovating my unfortunate wardrobe, as my
requirements were pressing. To prevent tres-
passing too much on your valuable space, I
will shortly narrate that I have had no less than
six persons recommended to me as needle-
women, or sempstresses, or whatever their
dignity allows them to be called, from three
different towns in the same county, and that

there was not one that had ever made a shirt,
though all had been brought up at various
schools; and the only result of my inquiries
has been the disheartening knowledge, that it
is impossible for me to obtain the services of
any one who would undertake to make a fine
shirt, although the population of the above-
mentioned towns averaged respectively 11,000,
6,000, and 2,000, and I was actually informed
that although, five years previously, the smallest
and most unimportant of these towns had possessed an admirable shirt-maker, who was also
a schoolmistress, that she had been removed
from her office, and had left the country, and
a successor had been appointed, who could
neither execute nor teach any manual arts,
employments, or occupations, beyond what the
wooden hook would accomplish, called by the
French name of *crochet*, and which (I was told),
on account of the great expense of fine-coloured
wools, was a much greater tax upon the parents,
than any benefit to the scholars! The person
who gave me the above information with
respect to the departed schoolmistress and

shirt-maker, lamented, as much as I did, the extinction of the art of making shirts, and added, that the *very names* of *trades and callings* were now changed, and that the *elegant nonentities* of the present day were *not* to be called *school-mistresses*, but " *governesses !* " Under these unhappy circumstances, my only resource is to beg for the benefit of your columns, to make known my present requirements, in the hope, that if any female still exists who can make a shirt, that she will be so obliging as to indicate the fact by advertisement in your paper, ad-dressed *to the gentleman in want of a shirt.* I am quite prepared to pay very handsomely, if my pattern is exactly followed.

I am, Sir,

Your obedient, humble Servant,

A GENTLEMAN IN DISTRESS.

POOR LAWS.

THE Hermit recounted an anecdote in reference to the effect of the Poor Laws as follows: —A poor man living on the side of the mountain about four miles distant died, after painful and lingering illness. He left a wife and two or three young children. It was the depth of winter, and the snow covered the ground. His wife inquired of the proper authority how she was to get a coffin, and was informed that she must go to the relieving officer, who lived nearly eight miles off, during which time she must have left the children in the house, or gone out of her way to reach the dwelling of a neighbour, where she might probably have found protection for them during her absence. Fourteen or sixteen miles in the snow, under great distress of mind, would be considered a heavy infliction for a man *under such circumstances*; but how much more for a woman? who possibly might not have found the relieving officer at home when she got to the end of her journey. In the present instance, the Hermit said, that the wretched poor woman thought that *he* might befriend her, and consequently she walked three miles in the snow to his cell (instead of eight), and obtained the poor boon she sought, viz. the Hermit's order for a coffin to be made for her husband's remains, with the risk of the parish refusing to pay for it had they been so disposed, because it was not commanded by the relieving officer ! Several other facts were mentioned by the Hermit, as having occurred under his own knowledge and that of his friend, sufficient to cause my exclamation of " Are we in a Christian country ? " and " Are these acts in *conformity* with the law ? *or punishable by the law ?* "

The Hermit believes that all these things are in conformity with the Poor Law Act, *if so,* why is such an Act suffered to exist without alteration and amendment? It also appears that great cruelty *can* be *legally* perpetrated with regard to the removal of poor persons who, notwithstanding a life of industry and an old age of honesty and virtue, are unable from bodily infirmity to gain any longer a sufficiency

for their own maintenance. The Hermit
mentioned one among many pitiful cases which
had been recounted to him by his rich and
benevolent neighbour. It was that of a
brother and sister who had always lived together, and, though the one was partially crippled
and the other was weak, they had managed to
earn their bread by their own exertions till they
were far advanced in years, when they were
necessitated to apply for parish relief. Upon
inquiry, it appeared that they belonged to a
parish more than one hundred miles distant,
although they had resided for so many years in
the locality where they had grown old, that
they were completely naturalized to the spot.
The parish authorities commenced a corre-
spondence, when, after months of wrangling
and delay, the distant parties decided that they
would not grant any relief unless the two old
people were sent to the workhouse more than
a hundred miles off, and they *were sent there !*

It appears that the Welsh have such a horror
of the workhouse, and are also naturally so very
kind-hearted, that numerous instances occur of

peasants and their wives, who earn their daily bread by hard labour, with children of their own, have brought up other children who have been put out to nurse with them after their parents have died, or have been unable to pay anything for their maintenance, rather than surrender them to the parish to be placed in a workhouse.

The Hermit has a horror of what is *now* called *centralization*. He says that the order of the Universe ought to teach mankind that everything is the centre of a small circle, and that it is contrary.to reason to suppose that human beings requiring various treatment, if collected together from various quarters in one place in a huge mass, can ever be properly cared for, managed, or attended.

On being informed of the enormous buildings now erected in towns for the purpose of receiving the poor from numerous parishes, he shuddered with horror at what he was convinced must necessarily be the dreadful results in various ways; and nothing could persuade him that if each parish, or perhaps two parishes, had a building appropriated for the reception of such persons as *ought properly* to be called "paupers," and if the remainder of the respectable industrious poor received such out-door relief as was proper under their various circumstances, that it would not only promote virtue and morality, but that it would render the perpetuation of great and long-continued abuses impossible, which must constantly occur in the overgrown communities I described, called "*Union Workhouses*," where all were strangers to each other, and where every tie was severed that was calculated to preserve the best characteristics appertaining to human beings, or Christians.

The Hermit described the Welsh workhouse that he recollected as existing in his own parish about half a century ago, which he then frequently visited. It was an old and spacious farm-house, situated on the edge of a wood by the side of a by-road, with a green before the door on which grew two large walnut trees. It was well supplied with running water, and it was selected as the workhouse for two parishes, the locality being convenient for both. It was kept by an old farmer and his wife, who were enabled to maintain two or three cows on the adjoining land ; and he well remembered the inmates of the establishment, of which he gave the following description :—On one of the hobs of the immense old-fashioned fire-place, which occupied a large portion of the side of the spacious kitchen, sat a man called Old Harry (yr hên Harri), who, from some injury, was unable to stand up, and could only move along the floor with his knees raised by means of his hands and feet. Old Harry was a most harmless individual, but he had outlived all his family, and was a proper object for admission into *what was then* a happy home for the inno-cent and really destitute poor. His pleasure was to be placed on the large stone hob in the recess of the chimney during cold weather, and to sit on the grass under the walnut trees in the warm weather. In the window of this kitchen, a Welsh woman of about fifty spun black wool at a large wheel. She had been for some years in a melancholy and half stupified state of mind; she had no one to maintain her, and had not sufficient command of intellect to maintain herself, but as long as she was provided with wool she was perfectly happy, and would spin from morning till night at the large wheel, which gave her exercise as well as occupation, and which lightened the expense of her maintenance.   A third member of this comfortable family was a crooked-looking, half-witted boy, called Billo.   He might then have been thirty years of age, but everybody looked upon Billo as a child; he was very short, but strong and honest, and he was allowed to go of errands for the neighbours, and carry small burdens, and assist the good man and his wife in the various proceedings of the farm.   Billo was a proper object for parish maintenance, as he also was deficient in bodily and mental ability to earn his own bread, although he could help those who ministered to his wants in many ways.

The Hermit added that he also recollected occasional additions, and a woman with little children, whose husband had run away from her, but she was not like a prisoner,—she

might have been supposed to have been a servant of the farm,—cheerful and bustling, she
took care of her own children, and was ready
to "lend a hand" to anything that was going
on; she was not separated forcibly from any
of her family, but she was thankful to find a
refuge within reach of her former home in the
time of need; and being near her friends, she
was very soon provided for, and enabled to
leave the workhouse for service, her relations
assisting in the maintenance of her children.

It now strikes me that the friends and relations
of persons who are sent to the workhouse would
exert themselves, in nine cases out of ten, for
the liberation of those within its walls, were
all workhouses *within easy reach* of their former
homes and connexions. "Out of sight, out of
mind," is a true saying. How few relations
of those immured in a workhouse *would*, or
could, go and see their friends, if ten, twenty,
or thirty miles off! And how few would fail
to do so, from the *weight of public opinion*, (*if
not* from affection), when each person in their
own locality would know whether they had

taken any notice of their distressed friends or relatives, or not!

On this subject I am a convert to the Hermit's theory of the benefit of *small circles,* each centre of which ought to govern its own especial native sphere, all being amenable to general laws; and I certainly read in the newspapers * of the present day enough to know that the workhouses are frequently, if not always, a *frightful conglomeration* of misfortune and misrule, generally accompanied by great cruelty. The management of such establishments can never properly be accomplished by any human beings (however great their talents, and however honest their intentions), without divisions and subdivisions, and the creation and multiplication of expensive departments now

---

* The appalling disclosures in the *Times* of this year (1866), relative to the sufferings occasioned from the treatment of the sick poor in certain workhouses, had not transpired when the Traveller made this note ; these disclosures have since proved that the Hermit did not err in the direful anticipations he entertained of the consequences of the present *monster* system, the *bare outline* of which was described to him by his guest.

unknown! but how much *more* natural, simple,
easier, and *better* would it be to let *each several
locality* have the care of its *own poor*, and thus
increase the number of responsible individuals,
and render available for the general good the
natural interests which must be, more or less,
awakened in the mind of each resident for the
fate and treatment of his own neighbours, and
which can only be secured by having workhouses
on a very moderate, not a *monster* scale, calculated
for the reception of the paupers of the place
who have no moral claim to out-door relief,
under the immediate and daily observation of
some one or other of the residents of the locality.
Doubtless the modern fallacy of supposing that
the *bigger* anything is—whether *monster* buildings, or *monster* meetings, or *monster* associa-
tions—the better it *must* be, is one of the great
mistakes of the present day, which time is
constantly developing, and which the Hermit
believes will appear more and more palpable as
facts are brought to light, to illustrate the study
of cause and effect. At present, I could have
told him, the aged and honest poor are con-

tinually *forced* into distant Unions, although
they only implore as much relief in money at
home as their maintenance would cost when
taken to the workhouse, but I *did not* tell him
this, because I could not in any way attempt to
defend a practice so totally unjustifiable, and
which ought to be illegal.

OATMEAL.

THE preparation of oatmeal is particularly
well understood in Wales, as well as in Scotland; but, by an extraordinary perversity, the
kilns necessary for its preparation are becoming
very scarce in the Principality, and in many
districts of South Wales the people are beginning to suffer very much from the kilns not
being kept up, or being appropriated to some
other use.   Next to *bread* and *good water*, oatmeal may be considered as one of the first
necessaries of life to a rural population; indeed,
in some parts of Wales it still (as in Scotland)
takes the place of bread in many instances; and
when this is not the case, its valuable and

nutritive properties, in sickness and in health, when it is converted into a variety of wholesome and nourishing dishes * by the Welsh, render it to them almost a staff of life; and yet, from the prevalent habit among the higher classes of ignoring or disregarding that which is in their power, many wealthy and philanthropic individuals are perfectly unconscious that the art of preparing oatmeal in Wales may be lost, and in some districts is almost extinct, in consequence of the kiln buildings being otherwise used, while the proprietor is paying a high price for oatmeal from shops which obtain that necessary article from Scotland, the purchaser being totally unconscious that oatmeal could be made to perfection by his own Welsh tenants.

The following amusing recipes for meagre dishes the Hermit allowed me to copy, after a conversation on the unwholesome nature and injurious effects of meagre cookery in general.†

DISH OF FROGS.

Take the thighs, and fry them in clarified
butter; then have slices of salt eel, watered,
flayed, boned, boiled, and cold; slice them in
thin slices, and season both with pepper, nutmeg, and ginger : lay butter on your paste, and
lay a rank of frog and a rank of eel, some
currans, gooseberries or grapes, raisins, pine-
apple seeds, juyce of orange, sugar, and butter;
thus do three times, close up your dish, and,
being baked, ice it.

Make your paste of almond, milk, flour, butter,
yolks of eggs, and sugar.

In the foresaid dish you may add fryed onions,
yolks of hard eggs, cheese-curds, almond-paste,
and grated cheese.

———————

TO MAKE A DISH OF MARROW.

Take the marrow of two or three marrow-
bones; cut it into pieces like great square dice,
and put to it a penny manchet, grated fine,
some slic't dates, half a quartern of currans,

a little cream, roasted wardens, pippins, or quinces, slic't, and two or three yolks of raw eggs; season them with cinamon, ginger, and sugar, and mingle all together.

***

DISH OF EGGS.

Take the yolks of twenty-four eggs, and strain them with cinamon, sugar, and salt; then put melted butter to them, some fine minced pippins, and minced citron: put it on your dish of paste, and put slices of citron round about it; bar it with puff paste, and the bottom also, or short paste in the bottom.

***

TO MAKE A DISH OF CURDS.

Take some very tender curds; wring the whey from them very well; then put to them two raw eggs, currans, sweet butter, rose-water, cinamon, sugar, and mingle all together; then make a fine paste with flour, yolks of eggs, rose-water and other water, sugar, saffron, and butter, wrought up cold : bake it either in this paste or in puff-paste; being baked, ice it with rose-water, sugar, and butter.*

The above recipes were extracted from a very curious work in the possession of the Hermit, by the celebrated Robert May, who published his " Accomplisht Cook; or, the Art and Mystery of Cookery. Dedicated to the Right Honourable my Lord Mountague, my Lord Lumley, my Lord Dormer, and the Right Worshipful Sir Kenelme Digby, so well known to this nation for their admired hospitalities." And in the Preface he says, that he values the " discharge of his own conscience in doing good " above all the malice of those who " make it their business to hide their candle under a bushel;" and he makes a solemn protest that he " has *not concealed any material secret*" of which he became possessed in fifty-five years' experience. He published his work in the year 1671.

---

* The digestive organs 200 years ago must have been very much stronger than in 1866, and did much credit to early hours, air, and exercise.

He was succeeded by William Rabisha, who published his " Cookery Dissected " in 1673, and dedicated his book to " Her Highness the illustrious Duchess of Richmond and Lenox, Her Highness the Duchess of Buckingham, Her Grace the Most Honourable renowned and singular good lady Lady Jane Lane, the Right Honourable good and virtuous Lady Mary Tufton, and the Hon. virtuous and good Lady Agnes Walker ; " and, among many wonderful compounds, both meagre, sweet, and savoury, the following, is entitled " *To Potch a Dish of Eggs for a Weak Stomach,*" and gives an idea of *lighter* lenten fare !

TO POTCH A DISH OF EGGS FOR A WEAK STOMACH.

A handful of good sorrel beaten in a mortar, strained with the juice of a lemon and vinegar ; put to it sugar and nutmeg ; take sippets, hardened upon a gridiron ; lay them on the bottom of your dish, put on them a little strong broth and a spoonful of drawn butter ; then pour in your sorrel, and set it on a great heap of coals.

Your eggs, being potched in a little water and salt, take them up, drain from the water, and lay them on your sippets; so cover them, and send them suddenly away. Your sauce must never be hotter on the fire than that you may eat it without cooling again; if you do, it will change the colour of your sorrel, and give your lemon a bad taste.

The following lines from Rabisha's work it ought to be the ambition of every good cook in the present century to *deserve* :—

> " ——— To show the nearest way
> To inform the lowest cook how she may dress
> And make the meanest meat the highest mess;
> To please the fancy of the daintiest dame,
> And suit her palate, that she praise the same."

———————

LUNCHEON.

I LATELY maintained a fierce argument with the Hermit on the word " Luncheon," which I said was often called " Lunch." The Hermit insisted upon it that no educated person in refined society could possibly talk of " Lunch,"

or " Lunching," but that they must always say
" Luncheon." I assured him that I had heard
persons who, from their birth and rank in life,
might be supposed to belong to refined society,
speak of "*Lunch*" instead of " *Luncheon,*" and
of " *Lunching*" instead of "*eating Luncheon,*"
and who said, " *I never Lunch,*" instead of " *I
never eat Luncheon.*" My good host, however, maintained that the origin of the word
was from " clutch " or " clunch," the meaning
of which was a *handful,* in contradistinction
to a *full meal*—a small quantity—to appease
hunger when there was no time to sit down to
the table ; and whether he is right or wrong, I
do not pronounce, but it was impossible to help
laughing when he said, " How would it be possible for a refined gentleman when he means to
imply that he has eaten a small quantity of
food in the *forenoon,* to exclaim, '*I clutched,*'
which," (added he,) " he might just as well say
as '*I lunched.*' Johnson himself quoted Gay as
authority for the word '*Luncheon.*' "

> "I sliced the *luncheon* from the barley loaf;
> With crumbled bread I thicken'd well the mess."

A RAINY DAY.

A LONG conversation upon the waste and mismanagement of the present age. The Hermit amused himself with making a calculation, founded upon the account I had given him,* of the number of extra meals and variety of food which it was the fashion to devour in the present day ; and, according to this statement, he said that the *overplus* of food, beyond what was required for health, taken by one individual, would, in one day, be sufficient to maintain one person and a half, giving as much as nature required for health : consequently, in each seven days more than ten human beings might be fed with the extra quantity that is now frequently taken by *one* to the detriment of his own constitution. This calculation was made without reference to the expense of various wines consumed by any one individual in the course of the week; as the Hermit drank nothing but water himself, he could not enter upon the latter point, and I was determined not to assist him, indeed, I half repented having given him the details I had already done with regard to eating; but had I supplied him with data upon which to base a calculation of the numbers that might be fed for the value of the quantity of wines which are drunk to the injury of health and the perpetuation of gout, I feared that he would make out so frighful a balance that it would disturb my mind, and I should not be able to sleep at night. I have hitherto taken care not to mention the modern practice of smoking to the Hermit, so very destructive to health; but I hardly suppose my host would believe me, if I gave details on this subject.

CONVERSATION WITH THE HERMIT,

On the Evils of Artificial Fattening of Cattle, to which he was violently opposed.*

ON referring to the above memorandum, I recollect that the Hermit's objections above recorded were expressed *long before* the outbreak of the Cattle Plague, since which time

I have extracted the following passages from
the pen of a gentleman * who was qualified,
surgically and medically, to pronounce upon
the actual consequences, as proved by his pro-
fessional examination of the wretched animals,
which were condemned to suffering and disease,
and were in that state pronounced to be first-
rate specimens of an art, creditable to science,
and to be encouraged for the good of mankind,
these poor diseased creatures being afterwards
sold for food! A calculation of the money
and time wasted to produce the diseased meat
of each of the prize specimens described in the
following paragraphs, would supply a singular
balance! And what is the result? *The Cattle
Plague!* And who can say that much disease
is not produced in human beings (if not the
cholera itself) by feeding upon such flesh?

" Certain bodily wants, when ill-suppressed,
are soon discovered. The air we breathe may
contaminate, but we can often smell, and
thereby avoid, an impure atmosphere. Our

---

* On the evil results of over-feeding cattle.   By Frederick
J. Gant, M.R.C.S. &c. &c.

clothing may be insufficient, but the wintry wind will soon warn us of this deficiency; a bilious head-ache instinctively prompts more active exercise, while fatigue suggests the necessity of repose. Air, temperature, exercise, and sleep are positive hygienic requirements, which severally proclaim their own demand when effective, and thus the tide of life flows smoothly on, each bodily want being wisely suggested by an appropriate, and almost unerring instinctive feeling. But it is otherwise with FOOD. True it is, that we eat when hungry, but this sensation does not prove an infallible guide in our choice of food, still less a criterion of its nutritive quality.

"When visiting the prize animals and others, lately exhibited at the Baker Street Bazaar, I took notes of my observations. One Devon cow looked very ill, and laid her head and neck flat on the ground, like a greyhound. I pointed out these animals to a man who was drawing water, and I asked him if their condition was one of common occurrence. He said, 'I knows nothing of them beasties, in p'ticler, but it's the case with many on 'em—I knows that.'

" I passed on to the pigs. A pen of three pigs happened to be placed in a favourable light for observation, and I particularly noticed their condition. They lay helplessly on their sides, with their noses propped up against each other's backs, as if endeavouring to breathe more easily; but their respiration was loud, suffocating, and at long intervals. Then you heard a short, catching snore, which shook the whole body of the animal, and passed, with the motion of a wave, over its fat surface, which, moreover, felt the cold. I thought how much the *heart*, under such circumstances, must be *labouring* to propel the blood through the lungs, and throughout the body! The *gold medal* pigs were in a similar condition—if anything, worse, for they snored and *gasped* for breath, their mouths being opened, as well as their nostrils dilated, at each inspiration; yet these animals, only twelve months and ten days old, were marked ' *improved* Chilton breed.'

Three pigs, of the black breed, were in a similar state at seven months, three weeks, and five days; yet such animals the judges '*highly commend.*'

" When I contrasted the enormous bulk of each animal with the small period in which so much fat, or flesh, had been produced, I naturally indulged in a physiological reflection on the high-pressure work *against time*, which certain vital internal organs, as the stomach, liver, heart, and lungs, must have undergone at a very early age. Now, with the best method of rearing cattle, or that which is most *conducive to their health*, the medical profession are only indirectly concerned; but of the *dietetic value* of animals so reared for food, the profession are, or should be, the immediate overseers and arbitrators.

" These were those to which the judges had awarded the highest prizes, as *specimens* of *healthy* rearing and feeding—viz., *the gold and silver medal prize bullocks, heifers, pigs, and sheep* (which remained in London).

" *This substitution of fat for muscle* is proved by the microscope to have ensued. For when thus examined, the muscular fibres no longer presented their characteristic cross markings, but the fibrillæ within the fibres were entirely broken up, and *replaced* by bright globules of *oily fat*. Each fibre contains an abundance of fat particles instead of fibrillæ within the fibre. The healthy structure of the heart had, therefore, thoroughly *degenerated* by the *substitution* of *fat* for muscle.

" Fortunately, the thin lining membrane (*endocardium*) had not been ruptured, or the animal would have *died instantly*. This might have happened at any moment, on the slightest exertion.

" *This animal, under three years of age, weighed upwards of two hundred stone, and was eating twenty-one pounds of oil-cake a day, besides other food.*

" Within about a foot of the termination of the large bowel was a putty-like mass, one inch and a half thick and about one foot long, and which partially surrounded the intestine. The mass consisted, apparently, of *scrofulous matter*.

" The fat referred to may itself be regarded as the superfluous food with which the animal had been gorged.

" The diseased condition thus produced may be termed *conversion* into fat, as expressive of the *apparent* change which has ensued; but, on closer examination with the microscope, I would ascribe the change itself to the *substitution* of fat (in the process of nutrition), for the *proper* structural elements—fibrillæ—of muscle, and not to the actual transformation of those elements into fat.

" We should, therefore, expect in vain to replenish our own muscles by the use of such food, nor should animals thus overfed be regarded as prize specimens of rearing and feeding. The heart being *converted into fat*, no longer retains its contractile power, but beats feebly and irregularly. The blood, therefore, now moves onward in a slow and feeble current. Hence the panting breathlessness due to stagnation of blood in the lungs, which the heart labours (in vain) to remove, while the skin and extremities are cold : hence the stupid heavy-headed expression of a congested brain, and the *blood-stained* appearance of meat after death. The slightest exertion of an animal under such circumstances might suddenly prove fatal. Were a man in this condition to present himself at an insurance office, it would *refuse* to insure his life at *any premium.* *Yet under similar circumstances a sheep is awarded gold and silver medals, and its feeder a prize of* 20*l. !*

" Under the present system the public have no guarantee, and are not ensured the best if indeed the cheapest food. The bulky withers of a fat bullock are no criterion of health, and its flat tabular back may conceal the revolting ravages of disease.

" The flesh of animals which has been produced by organs themselves diseased, is itself also necessarily *deteriorated*, and ought not to be regarded as prime samples of human food. These facts will be best understood by pathologists, but they also come home to the understandings, and certainly to the *stomachs* of *the people*. Nor can their feelings fail to respond to the claims of sympathy. The suffocating sighs of those fat pigs are an appeal to humanity.

" If offence come out of truth, it were better that the offence come, than that the truth be concealed."

MEM.*—Conversation with the Hermit about clipping horses, of which he had never heard. He was at a loss for the reasons which could have induced such an extraordinary proceeding. I *would* not tell him what I believed was the original cause, because it would have furnished him with another argument against the great progress of intellect in the present century, but I *do* believe that the real origin of clipping in the first instance was that horses might *appear* to be kept

in what is called " high condition," although
belonging to owners who could not afford such
expense, but that the practice gained ground
from the approval of the majority of those
whose duty it was to clean horses, and whose
labour was thereby much diminished, and
specious arguments were made use of to persuade masters that the animals themselves
benefited by such a course of treatment, as the
majority of masters possibly do not know how
horses ought to be treated any better than the
majority of mistresses of families (who have
cooks) know how to instruct them to prepare
food—but had I said this to the Hermit he
would have asked me whether I considered
that the stable management in Great Britain
generally was more indicative of the improvement of human intelligence than the culinary
department in the nineteenth century?   In
which case I must have answered " No," and
subjected myself to additional mortification.

WATER-FOUNTAINS.*

Mem.—Being fearful that I might have exaggerated the destitution of London with respect to water, I have, through a friend (while still in the cell of St. Gover) referred to documents belonging to the Metropolitan Free Drinking Fountain Association, which was established in 1859, and I find that I might have said much more, although I should have only thereby confirmed the Hermit's opinion that the progress of science has completely outrun the progress of the cultivation of *sense!*

There were no public drinking fountains in London till April, 1859. The water used in the metropolis amounts to one hundred millions of gallons, and, if formed into one reservoir, would form a lake seventy acres in extent, and six feet deep; yet every drop of this enormous supply must be paid for to water-companies, who, although by mechanical means they force water into the houses, make *no provision* for the wants of the multitudes who traverse the streets, and who are as much in want of a draught of water as the travellers of the desert. The resident poor suffer grievously in consequence of an intermittent supply of water, and the absence of free public street supplies ; and, although water-pipes are brought into the houses, it is turned on but once a day, seldom exceeding, and often for less than, half an hour ; and if they have any lack of vessels, or an accident occurs in spilling the water supplied during that short period, they must go *without water* till the next day, as it is *illegal even to buy it from any but the companies*—persons *giving water*, or *selling it* may be *prosecuted!* and every *drop of water* caught by the poor during the precious half hour that it is supplied after being kept in the fœtid atmosphere of a crowded dwelling, soon *becomes poisonous*, and water, which should be a preservative to life and health, is an actual source of fever and death. Under such circumstances, the pumps of London were the only places where many of the poor could obtain water to drink, which were few in number, and at great distances from each other, and in the investigation made of late years as to the cause of the epidemics which spread death and desolation in so many homes, the mischief was found to arise *as frequently* from the *water drunk* as from the air breathed, and the London pump-water was declared to be so impregnated with impure matter from the impurities of foul surrounding soil, that it was almost universally condemned. The Medical Officer of Health for the city of London * stated, that of thirty-six pumps in the City, scarcely one supplied water fit to drink, and the poor were left to choose between the poisonous water in the pumps, and the poisonous water stored up in their own tanks and cisterns.

The *only remedy* was public free drinking fountains, first established in London by Mr. Samuel Gurney, by whom the first drinking fountain was erected on Snow Hill in 1859, at which as many as five thousand people were known to drink in one day. Since 1859, eighty-nine drinking fountains, five cattle troughs, and some dog troughs have been

---

* Dr. Letheby.

opened by the Society, in addition to which between thirty and forty have been erected in London by private benevolence; and it is estimated in London alone more than *three hundred thousand people* drink daily at these fountains. But yet there are *whole parishes* still *without a single fountain*, and the sufferings that a vast multitude must still experience from thirst, and the horrible results to thousands now ruined in body and soul, occupants of lunatic asylums and prisons, whose state has been caused by being *forced* into public houses and gin palaces to supply their *daily thirst*, is dreadful to contemplate in a Christian country, whilst the sufferings of the poor cattle, sheep, and dogs, are intolerable from the want of supplies of drinking troughs for animals; and the subscriptions of charitable individuals are not sufficient to do a tithe of the work which is still required to place fresh water within the reach of all the poor in London, to whom, as well as to every other class, the sight of running water is in itself a gratification. Running water also serves to clear away any obstruction which might otherwise choke up the overflow pipe, and any supply of water which could only be obtained by turning a cock would *not* answer the purpose required.

A force of police is required specially to protect the fountains, for, in the present corrupt and demoralized state of society, constant supervision is necessary to preserve them from injury. Drunken men are their determined enemies, cups are stolen and taken away, sticks are thrust into the jet, and stones, pipe, rope, buttons, and orange-peel are also frequently used to render them inconvenient or useless, and thus it has been found that fountains erected in London by private benevolence have been so injured that the charitable donors have found they must submit to the expense of keeping their fountains in order, or see their good intentions defeated. The fountains in the care of the Society are alone rendered a permanent blessing by the visits of their own officers of the Society, who regularly inspect them, report their condition, and have damages immediately repaired.

An interesting article by Dr. Wynter contains the whole history of the water supply of London, from the time when the metropolis was interspersed with meadows, and supplied with water from its bournes, its viaducts, and its wells; and when the Thames was a clear river, free from all the impurities that have now converted it *into one great sewer*, until Peter Morris, the Dutchman, obtained a right from the Corporation of London to erect machinery for that purpose in 1580, after which Sir Hugh Middleton proposed to bring a new river into London, from the springs of Chadwell and Amwell, a distance of forty-two miles, when no forcing apparatus was made use of, which system continued till 1782, when water-pipes were carried underground in every direction, and forced up to the top stories, since which time eight water-companies supply the metropolis, and

> " Water, water, everywhere ;
> But not a drop to drink."

When the Legislature forced all the water-companies supplying themselves from the

Thames, higher up the stream, it never anticipated the evils which are now apparent. The towns on the banks of the Thames above the highest sources from which any of the water-companies now obtain their supplies, have obtained permission to *drain directly into the river*, and, instead of going up the stream to get nearer the pure element, they are only meeting the refuse and drainage of these towns half-way.

N.B. I *dared not* tell the Hermit that I had heard before I ever saw him, that the favourite and fashionable theory now promulgated, for curing all the evils entailed by want of water in London, is to convey the pure element from the Bala Lake, in North Wales, into the metropolis,—of course *without* the slightest regard to the *robbery* of the *Principality*, or of the injury (to say nothing of the disfigurement) which would result to the inhabitants of that beautiful locality, and were the scheme *not* so very wild, were the expense *not* so very enormous, and were the distance *not* so very great, there would be a probability that it might not be attempted! but as it appears to involve every possible objection, there is cause for the greatest alarm, as the disposition of the present generation is to revel in the excitement of undertakings, which are certain to ruin their projectors, and to materially injure a large portion of the rest of mankind.

Dr. Wynter, however, has committed himself to the opinion, that London may rival Glasgow, which is said to have the purest water in the world, without robbing poor Wales, or going to the enormous expense of bringing water from a Lake in the Principality to London, as water may be had of a pure quality, and in abundant supply, from the gathering grounds which supply the town of Farnham in Surrey. If this is the case, the Hermit might justly say, it is another proof of the proneness of the present age of education and science, to go a hundred miles out of the way, and to spend a thousand times more than is necessary to obtain what is, comparatively speaking, to be found close at hand, but which for that reason is not valued.

The curse of London is certainly want of water, and drunkenness! How has this curse been brought upon London? By the *voluntary acts of mankind!* by the want of reflection, and the consequent misapplication of mechanical talent, under the name of " *Improvements*," in the nineteenth century.

It seems to me, *since I have begun to think*, that there are several words which have been so long and continually used in the wrong sense, that people are in danger of forgetting their real signification, viz. the destruction of fine old churches, and the construction of modern paltry buildings on their site, is called " *Restoration;* " whilst the words " Ignorance " or " Barbarism," are now applied to those who have retained the knowledge transmitted by their ancestors, of the useful arts of every-day life. Sophistication is called *education*, and a " *superior education* " implies the wilful neglect of instruction in all useful knowledge.

HOLLY—MISTLETOE—IVY.*

In a conversation with the Hermit, in which I gave him some idea of Arboriculture (as at present practised) in many "*highways* and *byways*," especially as connected with Holly in hedges, I omitted to mention the barbarous and ignorant practice (where a standard holly *has* been preserved) of cutting all the branches off close to the stem, up to the top, where a few boughs only are permitted to remain, giving that beautiful tree exactly the appearance of a *besom* set up on end, and which disfigurement is incurable, because the holly-tree never puts out new branches when cut close to the stem.

It is very strange that the propagation of the Mistletoe is not better understood — its beauty, independent of its medical properties,† as well as its traditional and historical interests, ought to cause its natural history to be more studied, and, consequently, better known ; but perhaps it is less extraordinary that this should have been neglected than that the IVY, which, in all its beautiful varieties, is more or less known in every part of Great Britain, should be the object of such *universal persecution*. The Hermit mentioned a fact relating to the ivy, with which I was previously unacquainted, and which I do not believe is generally known, although it is in the power of everybody to see and observe, viz., that when it attains a certain age, and is peculiarly ornamental to the tree on which it hangs, it *ceases* to throw out feelers; consequently, that the outcry that when ivy is old its stem must be cut through, or it will *destroy the tree*, is one of the most remarkable hallucinations of the present age. When ivy is old, it *ceases* to be attached to the stem round which it is twisted, excepting by its folds, which are so completely loose from the stem of the tree that a hand may be frequently passed between the ivy and the tree, while the upper boughs are supported by festoons from branch to branch; consequently, if the ivy is merely thinned sufficiently *above* (when it becomes top-heavy), to prevent too great a weight upon the small boughs of the tree, it cannot in any way injure the tree; and yet ivy, in the state above described, appears to be a favourite mark for the axe to sever. The Hermit pointed out to me several beautiful evergreen trees in the winter, which at a distance I did not identify to be ivy, and I wondered what bright and shining standard evergreens thus enlivened his wood; but he explained that these verdant objects were simply produced by planting ivy (or preserving it when wild) to grow up dead trees, which, being at length entirely covered, resembled standard evergreens of the most brilliant tint. I agree with the Hermit that a series of experiments might be made, with interesting and useful results, to ascertain at what age ivy *ceases* to adhere to the tree against which it grows,—also, the different characteristics of the various sorts of ivy. The Hermit is of opinion that the *very diminutive* wild ivy, which grows especially on walls, the stem of which seldom attains any bulk, and which forms a beautiful network all over the stones, is a great preservative to mason-work, and ought to be specially planted and encouraged against park-walls, in preference to the ivy, generally called Irish, which, however, is not believed to be indigenous in that country.

ROADS, HEDGES, AND BANKS.*

I HAVE had a conversation with the Hermit, on the present frequent *mis*management, and actual *destruction* of live fences, on the sides of high-ways and byways, but he was so anxious that I should return to my lessons in the *culinary* art, that he did not then give me time to tell him the anecdote I was about to narrate, of the discovery of a friend of mine, as to the immediate cause of the miserable system by which the banks, on the sides of roads, are so maltreated, that the hedges and roadside timber are frequently *undermined* ; but he afterwards requested me to write it down, and to illustrate it with my pencil,† and expressed his opinion that if I placed the narra-tive in my Note Book, with the sketches, it might some day be of service to those whose property is annually destroyed, while the public safety is endangered, but who either have not opened their eyes to see the evil done, or their understandings to prevent it.

My friend was a landholder, of considerable property, who, having gone abroad for his health, had heard nothing of what had taken place in his own parish for more than twelve months, and on his return he could scarcely recognise the roads around his home. When he went away, there was fine roadside timber, including splendid hollies, and substantial hedges, growing on firm and solid banks— when he returned, it appeared as if an *invading army* had devastated the whole of the environs. The fine and flourishing hedges were cut down to within a short distance of the top of the bank, so as to remove every impediment to bipeds or quadrupeds going over it with ease. The previous winter had been very severe, and the snow had frozen on the small remnant of growing sprays left, so that few and sickly shoots had been brought forth in the summer, which shoots had been quickly disposed of by the cattle and sheep, who, after they had eaten up the few leaves left, amused themselves with looking over into the road, and occasionally making a descent upon it, over the slight obstacles in their way, which an active boy could have cleared with one bound; and which the quadrupeds walked over, or burst through with the greatest ease.*

My friend was shocked and distressed by the general disfigurement, and the aspect of barren misery which such a prospect entailed; but being a person of intelligence, he soon discovered that it was *not alone* by wilful and ill-judged cutting down, that such a very rapid decadence of hedges had been produced, but that the *banks* had been *cut away*, and pared down, and *scooped into*, in such a manner, that the natural nourishment of the hedges had been abstracted; and with regard to the hedge-timber, the excavation of the banks had been carried on to such an excess, that the trees had been undermined, and their roots cut through and exposed on the side next the road; whilst

the banks in other places being sliced down per-
pendicularly, the roots of the hedge-timber, as
well as the live hedges, were not only visible to
the naked eye, but protruded in some instances,
horizontally, three or four inches beyond the
surface of the soil.

My friend followed up his investigations,
until he made out that in his locality, the
following causes had led to these most lament-
able results, and to injuries, which could not
be remedied for many years, so as to restore or
renew what had been so wantonly destroyed.
The causes were as follows :—

The farmers were annoyed by the unusual stir
which had followed the appointment of new
road surveyors ; and though they might not have
been totally insensible to the disfigurement of
their premises, were certainly more keenly aware
of the time that had been occupied in cutting
down their fences, according to the orders of
the new officers, which officers seemed to have
had but one idea, viz. that the more completely
the hedges were destroyed, and the roads rendered unsightly, and destitute of shade or

shelter, the greater would be the appearance of their own activity, and the greater credit they would obtain.   Of the *roads* themselves, very little notice was taken, excepting to allow those employed upon them, to excavate gutters under the banks, and to scrape as much of the surface away from the *sides* of the road, as to render them so convex as to occasion frequent overturns, when vehicles passed each other in the dark,—in short to imitate the shape of a saucer turned upside down.

My friend was convinced that some party or parties must have an especial motive for these latter proceedings, which were equally subversive of the interests of the public, and positively injurious to private individuals, and he found that the explanation of the whole was as follows. The roads had long been neglected, but the hedges were excellent, though they might have been in some places a little too redundant, and required the moderate pruning of any sprays which protruded over the road so as to interfere with loaded corn-waggons. An outcry for mending the roads was raised in the neighbourhood. The new officials ("*highways*" and "*byways*") found the repairs needed (viz. picking up and stoning and making coffer gutters) troublesome, expensive, and tedious, and they thought that if they could produce a rapid transformation by means of cutting down hedges and making *brooms* of the roadside timber, this startling effect would, by the sudden change, impress the public with the reality of "great improvement." Moreover, as they ordered the farmers to be the executioners of their own hedges, their destruction involved no expense, and did not create any extra items in the books,—another advantage so far as the officials were concerned, but the misplaced industry of the race so called "road-menders," was *not* solely attributable to the supervisors, but also to the blindness of the farmers themselves to their own interests, having forgotten the old adage of "robbing Peter to pay Paul," as he discovered that the farmers often gave money or beer to the road-menders (employed by the Highway or By-way surveyors) for slicing down the banks next.

the road upon which their own hedges grew, by which they believed they were enriching themselves by means of their *enemy's troops*, whereas for every cartload of soil thus obtained by the loss of the banks, they entailed upon themselves the expense of incessant mending and repairing hedges *until quite dead*, and afterwards of keeping up a dead fence without any " tenet " * at hand. It was truly " killing the goose with the golden egg," for between the road-surveyors and road-menders and farmers, the Irish notice might have been practically rivalled, and instead of the sign-post in the Emerald Isle, which announced that " The *improvements* on Market Hill rendered the roads *impassable*," there might have been a notice, " Beware of bulls and other horned animals, as in consequence of the repair of the roads, all live fences have been destroyed and all banks carried away or undermined."

This anecdote, I fear, is not a solitary instance, nor is it exaggerated, but the Hermit laughed aloud when he heard it, and said, gaily,

---

* A word used for the loppings of brushwood used to repair dead hedges.

" What can you expect but *such improvements* as long as a modern education is confined to the various arrangements of the letters of the alphabet, without thought or reflection or any regard to palpable facts under the eye? Do you suppose that if any three persons (or perhaps one) in your friend's neighbour-hood, had used either their eyes or under-standings, and resolutely and perseveringly opposed this destructive mischief while in its course, on its *true grounds*—that it could not have been stopped? Of *course it could*, but it seems, by your own account, that half the world are blind, and the other half cripples, in mind at all events, if not in body."

WALL-FLOWERS.

I HAVE observed that the top of every wall near the Hermit's abode is surmounted by wall-flowers, the wild single sort, which are always the most fragrant, and among which an endless variety of tints are observable from the young plants which spring up spontaneously every

year, self-sown afresh, and the Hermit pointed
out some of a violet colour, so that had I not
examined the flowers, I should have believed
they belonged to another species of plant; but
my host confessed that although wall-flowers
grew wild in the locality of his abode, that he
had saved the seeds and sown, not only the tops
of *all* his own walls, but those of *all* his neighbours, which proceeding, he added, had produced the greatest amount of innocent pleasure
to the greatest number of persons at the
smallest expense and trouble, of anything that
he had ever done. He added that this idea
had originated from reflecting upon the bounti-
ful supplies of Providence with regard to wild
flowers, of which, he was surprised to find from
my statements that so little was thought in the
present great world, and that many valuable
species of plants were almost extinct from
being persecuted as weeds, and he thought he
would try the above experiment where at all
events no one would be injured. Its success
was beyond his expectations, and not only did
he himself revel in the increased beauty and

fragrance of his wild *wall-garden*, but he was gratified to find that his poorer neighbours, in fact every one who passed within sight or smell of these delightful flowers, expressed their gratification. A year or two afterwards he added the seeds of the red and yellow antirhinum (or snapdragon), which had succeeded equally well, and added to the beauty of his wild wall garden without requiring any other nourishment than that bestowed by heaven.

SHEEP'S MILK.

I CONFESS that when the Hermit first told me that his best cheese owed its superiority to the addition of sheep's milk, I thought he was jesting; and although I saw the ewes being milked, and admired the Arcadian scene, I supposed, in my ignorance, that the milk was to *feed the calves!* But I am now fully aware that the milk of that valuable animal (the Welsh sheep), when mingled with that of the cow, produces cheese which is not only excellent to eat new, but, when old, is more like Parmesan than anything else I ever tasted.

The following are memoranda of facts relative to the Hermit's flock of Welsh sheep:—

His lambs were sold when I was with him, about the beginning of July, at 1*l.* each, being then from three to four months old. The ewes were then milked for three months. They were twenty-four in number, and they gave on an average twenty-four quarts a day. The proportions for cheese were one quart o ewe's milk to five quarts of cow's milk, and six quarts of ewe's milk to thirty quarts of cow's milk made a cheese, weighing from twelve to fourteen pounds, of a most superior quality, with the sharpness so much admired in Parmesan. Some of these ewes became so fat after they were dried in October, that when they were killed at Christmas, their weight was from fourteen to fifteen pounds a quarter, and the mutton of the very finest flavour. Of course there was *no stall-feeding*, or *confinement*, or *quackery* with artificial food, but only pastures, often changed, and a good shed to run into at pleasure. The Hermit seldom or ever lost a lamb, but his sheep were supplied with chaff and cut roots in winter, when there was not sufficient grass to support them well.

To give an idea of the profit of Welsh sheep when properly managed, I have made a note of the profits of ten of the Hermit's Welsh wethers, which were *bought* the *latter end of March,* and sold the beginning of the following May; their price was 1*l.* 10*s.*, and they were sold at 2*l.* off turnips. It is also to be remembered that the Welsh wool is a very fine quality, and peculiarly well adapted for cloth as well as flannel, and those native Welsh cottagers who are still wise enough to make use of their wool-wheels, produce a home-spun cloth which, like the brocades of old, is so durable that they may almost be considered as heir-looms. The home-knit Welsh stockings of the black Welsh sheep's wool, are also very superior, and do not need any dye. I also observed that the Hermit's flock was so tame that they followed the shepherd about, and some of them would eat out of his hand, and on remarking that I had always been told the Welsh sheep were so wild that it was impossible to keep them within bounds, I was informed that there was not the slightest inconvenience in keeping Welsh sheep if they were *properly managed*, but that if purchasers chose to go to Welsh fairs or markets, and bought sheep of different flocks, drove them to a strange place, and then took no precautions to reconcile them to their new locality, they would be very likely to find the next morning that their sheep had all disappeared in different directions ; but that if a flock was purchased that had been accustomed to live together, and if they were at first placed in a well-fenced pasturage with plenty to eat, they would soon become reconciled to the change, but when born and brought up on the same spot, they never wished to stray. In short, it appears that Welsh sheep exactly resemble the Scotch Highland cattle—if untamed, untended, uncared for, they are as unmanageable as wild beasts, but when domesticated they are mild, docile, and have no

inclination to wander. The Welsh sheep certainly is one of the most *symmetrical* animals I
ever beheld, and appears to particular advantage
when black, their arched necks, slender legs,
small, compact, and well-proportioned, bodies,
their long graceful tails, and picturesque curling
horns, with their soft dark fleeces and brilliant
dark eyes, would render them fit studies for
Rosa Bonheur.

GOATS.

The Hermit's Welsh Goats were differently
managed to those I have seen on the Continent, and they are much handsomer animals
than the foreign goats, with which I am
acquainted. It is surprising that no specimen
of the real Welsh goat is preserved in the
Zoological Gardens. The Welsh goat being
an aboriginal of Britain, ought to be specially
protected, whereas it appears that the breed is
likely to become extinct. The gallant regiment of
the Welsh Fusiliers ought to protest against this

neglect of an animal which has always been associated with Welsh regiments and the Principality of Wales.

The Welsh goat has a very picturesque appearance, from its long coat and beautifully formed head. There are two species equally aboriginal; one with magnificent horns, and the other without horns. The Hermit had both kinds, and he made a point of keeping as many as he could without horns, because they were not dangerous to the numerous peasant children who were continually playing with them. The Hermit said that his goats certainly had a predilection for the bark of young trees, and he therefore for many years had adopted the plan of tethering them. Each goat was provided with a leather collar and chain, one end of which was attached by a ring to the leather strap which forms the collar, and at the other end there was a ring which was fastened to the ground by a sharp wooden hook. The goats seemed perfectly happy, their chains were very long, and they were moved twice or thrice a day. They were always brought into a large yard at night, where they were left at perfect liberty, with an open shed where they had prunings of shrubs or vegetables or anything that was convenient, given them to eat. The she-goat gives when in full milking *more* than *two quarts* a day. The value of their milk for children and invalids has been admitted in all ages ; their milk makes excellent cheese alone, without the mixture of any other, and the whey is particularly nourishing and wholesome, as well as the curd which is produced a second time from boiling the whey. Kids are always marketable, being excellent food, and their skins very valuable.

FEATHERS.

THE Hermit had a great horror of a feather bed, which, he said, had been caused by observation of the dreadful consequences to invalids, or those who were bedridden, of lying in a *hot hollow*, instead of having a flat cool elastic surface to repose upon, and likewise from knowing that feathers caused, absorbed, and retained

perspiration, and consequently that under any
circumstances they were the most objectionable
material that could be selected, either for health
or convenience, to be lain upon by rich or poor.
Feathers, however, seemed to be very much
valued in his establishment, and they were carefully preserved and cured in the following
manner.

All the feathers were plucked into empty
boxes, kept in an outer building, and it was the
business of an aged widow, who had nothing
to do with the culinary department, as soon as
her box was full, to put them into a large high
tub which had previously been filled with lime-
water, made by putting hot lime into another
tub overnight, and filling it up with water,
stirring it well, and leaving it to stand for
twelve hours, after which, the lime being pre-
cipitated to the bottom, the clear lime-water
was poured off into the tub in which the
feathers were to be immersed, and which being
stirred round with a stick, were left to soak for
four and twenty hours, at the end of which
time the quill of every feather would have

burst or cracked at the end in which the animal oil is contained, which has so offensive and unhealthy a smell in feathers imperfectly cured. The feathers were then taken out and put into common washing-tubs, where they were washed in warm water with a little soft soap, and then a sheet being spread over a large empty tub, the water with the feathers was ladled out into the sheet, and the water having drained away, the feathers were placed thinly upon a dry sheet, which was put upon a square frame (or *cratch*) composed of thin strips of wood nailed together, and fixed on the top of four upright sticks in the sun (if in summer), or else suspended to four hooks fastened in the ceiling of the Hermit's kitchen in winter. As soon as the feathers were dry, they were taken away by the featherwife, who stripped them, cutting off the hard part of the quill with a pair of scissors, and by practice she was so expert, she almost mechanically placed in their respective heaps the finer and the coarser down, which at the end of the day she put in paper bags and hung along the beam of the ceiling.

This occupation is particularly well adapted for old women, who can sit near a fire, and pursue this employment in the winter, as a means of subsistence. The Hermit had a little building on purpose, where there was a good fireplace, and a long beam for the feather-bags; the contents of which were perfectly sweet, and as downy and *fluffy*, as if they had never been wetted. They were appropriated to making quilts for the winter and pillows.

The Hermit said that it was not from the custom of his country he had learnt this, as he must admit that the Welsh were *too fond* of feather-beds; but that although he did not wish to introduce the *rolling balloons* of the Germans, called Eider-down quilts, he thought that much gratitude was due to that nation, for the sensible idea of putting feathers over instead of under human beings in the winter.

The Hermit's bedsteads had strips of wood at the bottom (*no sacking*), on these were placed a very deep, but very soft mattress, filled with oat-straw, or beech-leaves, but not those dreadful inventions, called by the French name of

" *Palliasse*," although never seen in that country. These mattresses had two openings in the seams, by which means the straw or leaves could be levelled by the hand every day, and the contents could be changed every year, or oftener if necessary, in the course of half an hour. Over a mattress of this description, a wool mattress was placed, with a small quantity of horse-hair, mixed with the wool in the centre, to increase the firmness and elasticity. Feather pillows completed the equipment of the bedding; and the upper, as well as the lower mattresses, were all made at home, and consequently easily re-made when necessary.

MOLES.

THESE little animals were special favourites of the Hermit, who said that they ought to be preserved for their utility, as well as protected for their harmlessness. He considered that their hillocks, of the finest earth, were an excellent top-dressing for grass, and that half the money spent in paying mole-catchers would be much more profitably bestowed in paying for spreading the mole-hills at dawn of day. I suggested that if moles were never destroyed, they might become so numerous as to get into his garden, and throw up their mounds over the young plants. He said, in that case they must be kept under and it would be only necessary to kill them in certain restricted localities, and these would be exceptional, but that the usual way of trapping them by letting them fall into deep empty boxes, out of which they could not crawl, and leaving them to die of famine, was a disgrace to humanity. The Hermit did not like my remark that their fur was as fine, if not finer, than sealskin, as he was afraid it might lead to a still further destruction of his favourite little underground ploughmen, and insect - destroyers ; and, he added, if the undeniable talent for mechanics which characterised the present age had not yet invented a merciful method of putting these innocent little animals to death when *no* benefit was derived by their flesh or skins, that nothing was to be expected but an increase of cruelty, if any profit was to be obtained from the latter. I informed him of the existence of the excellent Society for the "Prevention of Cruelty to Animals," and he asked me, "how it was that all these years it had *forgotten the moles?*" which question I could not answer.

BEES.

THE Hermit has a large establishment of bees, to which industrious insects he is not only particularly partial, but he has a sort of respect, I might almost say *reverence*, for them, which is very general among his country-men, and which surprised *me*, although he appeared to be *as much* surprised at my know-ing so little about their habits or their treatment; but still I was able to inform him that there were in England many scientific Apiarians, who had made the treatment of bees their especial study. He asked me whether the study had led to a great increase of bee-keepers in England generally, but I told him that the houses or *boxes* recommended for their abode were so very expensive, and required such very neat joiners' or cabinet-makers' work, that it was impossible to expect that any but those in affluent circumstances could keep bees; this unfortunate remark has brought a storm down upon my devoted head, as I unfortunately furnished my host with a new argument in support of his opinion, that everything he hears from me proves that the present age is anything but an age of common sense.

There is, however, no doubt that the Hermit's bees thrive remarkably well, and that so far from their houses or their management being complicated or expensive, they are neither one nor the other; and for the benefit of my friends, I have made sketches of the hives,* which are all double, a small one at the top, and a large one at the bottom. It appears that the bees fill the top hive for the Hermit, and make further provision for themselves in the lower hive.

No. 1.   Top Hive (on its Mat), 6 inches high, and 10 inches diameter.
   2.   Mat, 11 inches diameter ; Hole, 2 inches in circumference.
   3.   Lower Hive (without Top Hive), 11 inches high, 16 inches in
         diameter, with Hoop 3 inches wide.
   4.   Lower and Upper Hive together, Mortared round the Hoop.
   5.   Wooden Scoop.
   6.   Jug for Keeping Bees' Winter Food, with Flat Top to be tied
       over.   TOTAL VALUE OF THE WHOLE . . 4s.

In the month of July, the Hermit takes off the top hive, which is generally full of the finest honeycomb. He replaces it with another the same size, leaving the contents of the lower hive undisturbed. The lower hive has a flat top, with an extra round of straw on the outer rim, within which the upper hive fits, and the hole in the centre of the top of the lower hive admits the bees from one to the other. There is a simple hoop of wood at the bottom of each of the lower hives, which the Hermit had neatly mortared round outside, so that there could be no egress into the hive, for any insects besides the bees themselves, who entered by one small aperture cut purposely in the hoop. Everything else was made of straw, worked in the usual beehive fashion, roll upon roll of straw, fastened together with strips of thin willow.

The Hermit had fifty double hives. I requested one of the widows to weigh a small top hive *empty*, and another of the same size *full*. The empty hive weighed one pound and a half; the full hives six pounds and a half; consequently at the rate of five pounds for the

owner's share, my host's bees produced an
average of two hundred and fifty pounds of
honeycomb, all filled with the purest honey, for
there never is either bee-bread or young bees
in the upper hives. I was informed that there
is no absolute necessity for the round mat of
straw which I observed under each of the top
hives, though it was convenient and useful, as the
hive was more easily lifted off without disturb-
ing the bees below, in a manner which would
not be the case if the upper hive rested only on
the top of the lower hive, without having any
independent platform; and as bees carefully
fill up every crevice which admits light, or
might give admission to insects, the upper
hive is generally cemented round the edge to
whatever it is placed upon, and therefore
to take it off suddenly produces a great
wrench and disturbance throughout the establishment, entirely avoided by the little mat,
which, having a hole in the middle answering
to the hole in the top of the lower hive,
admits the bees from one to the other. When
the bees swarmed, they were hived in the

lower hive, and the hole at the top had a cork in it; but the evening after (if they had settled quietly) the cork was withdrawn, and the top hive with its mat put in its proper place, and as soon as the bees were thoroughly at home, the hoop of the lower hive was mortared round with a trowel, after dark, a piece of white paper, pricked full of holes, being placed over the entrance attached by four pins to the hoop (while the above operation was performed), to prevent the bees from coming out.

The Hermit's bees were always fed from the month of November, till the spring blossoms rendered it no longer necessary. Their food was so inexpensive that the Hermit never permitted the question of their being sufficiently provided with their own honey to prevent their having the offer of *supper* every night, during the period above mentioned, as he said that, if they did not require it, they would not eat it, but it very seldom happened that they did not take the whole quantity, except in very hard frosts, when they are in a state of torpor.

Their food consisted of treacle, in the proportion of one teacupful to two of water, boiled together, in a jug plunged in a saucepan of boiling water, with as much salt sprinkled in as gave it the very slightest saline flavour.*
This mixture was kept in jugs with narrow spouts and flat tops, over which thick brown paper was tied, to keep out the dust; and every night two of the widows went to each hive, with a candle, the jug of boiled treacle and water, and scoops made of elder or other wood, which they placed in the mouth of each hive, leaving the portion outside which was not hollowed. They filled each scoop with as much of the prepared food as the cavity would hold without overflowing. The first thing in the morning the scoops were withdrawn, and, being well washed, were put to dry in the house, on a shelf, till the following night. If the bees left any of their food in the scoop, it was not washed out, but withdrawn during the day, and replaced the next night in the hive from which it had been taken.

When the spring is sufficiently advanced for the bees no longer to require food in the hive, they will not take it; but as the weather is very uncertain, and the sun and a few flowers may tempt them out for two or three days, after which a change may take place, to prevent their obtaining any food abroad, the Hermit's widows were frequently obliged to recommence feeding between the end of February and April. The Hermit explained that feeding the bees not only kept them strong and vigorous, but that it saved a great deal of time with regard to their labours in the spring; as, if they had a good stock of honey for their own use, they begun the sooner to work for their master, and in good years the top hive may be changed twice between June and September.

The Hermit was very indignant at the idea of joiner's work or cabinet-maker's work being necessary to make houses for bees; and he said there was no greater mistake than to suppose that bees could only thrive under one aspect; — that a little observation might convince any one interested in the subject that bees will

thrive in various aspects, provided they are
sheltered from wind, and they have easy access
to pure but shallow water, where they can
drink without danger of being drowned; also
that where the locality will not admit of a safe-
watering-place for the bees, fresh water should
be placed twice or thrice a day in shallow pans,
in the shade, near the bee-house, which, if possible, should have a projecting roof of stone-
tile to screen them well from the rays of the sun.

A little penthouse of this description, built
against the wall, with the ends boarded or
bricked up with a shelf from end to end (which
shelf ought to be about an inch from the back
wall), is quite sufficient for all useful purposes
connected with bees. If stone-tile cannot be
had, the roof should have double boards as a
protection against the sun, and it should be
plastered inside, and whitewashed inside and
out every year, and frequently swept between
the hives and examined, to see that no ants or
snails, or other insects or reptiles, have taken
up their abode in the bees' dominions, which is
often the cause of their deserting their hives.